Sturgeon Moon

Also By Robert Lavett Smith

Everything Moves With A Disfigured Grace
Smoke In Cold Weather: A Gathering of Sonnets
The Widower Considers Candles

"Smith's gift lies in the ability to explore sorrow without being maudlin and in the not seeming constrained even when voluntarily constraining himself to classical poetic forms like the sonnet. Indeed, it's easy to forget, while reading his musings, that they *are* sonnets, so natural is the language. He's equally at home with free verse, as demonstrated in the chapters of the life of Reverend Igneous Rock—a sardonic character destined, in my opinion, to achieve literary immortality."

—Jeff Kalmar, songwriter and guitarist

"In 'Daybreak In Alabama,' his response to the Langston Hughes poem of the same name, Robert Lavett Smith confronts, as he so often does in his work, the contradictory forces of joy and pain that are always implicit in life:

. . .there are days
when night gains the upper hand
even in skies so cloudless and clear
you can taste the ripe light on your tongue.

Smith has an appropriate name, because he *is* quite a wordsmith. He takes what is simple and straightforward in the world and somehow makes it eloquent. *Sturgeon Moon* is a great piece of writing."

—Buford Buntin, author of
Love, War, and Other Considerations

STURGEON MOON

Robert Lavett Smith

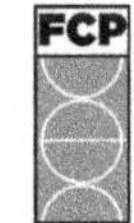

Full Court Press
Englewood Cliffs, New Jersey

First Edition

Published in the United States of America
by Full Court Press, 601 Palisade Avenue
Englewood Cliffs, NJ 07632
fullcourtpressnj.com

ISBN 978-1-938812-93-4
Library of Congress Control No. 2017937243

Book Design by Barry Sheinkopf for Bookshapers (bookshapers.com)

Author Photo by Laurie Sato

FCP Colophon by Liz Sedlack

Cover art courtesy istockphoto.com

In memory of Dr. C. Lavett Smith, 1927–2015

"Lifting the valleys of the sea
my father moved through griefs of joy;
praising a forehead called the moon. . . ."

—e.e. cummings, "My Father Moved Through Dooms of Love"

ACKNOWLEDGMENTS

The author wishes to thank the following publications, both in print and online, in which some of these poems first appeared, occasionally in slightly different versions:

Aegis: "The Flower Burning"; "If I Had My Druthers"; "Lullaby and Dirge"; "*Scène de Genre*"; "The Wedding"

Big River Poetry Review: "Our Parents May Be Clinically Insane"

The Cream City Review: "Fickle Weather"

Dead Snakes: "At My Father's Deathbed"; "Beyond the Veil"; "The Colossi"; "Dad Didn't Waste His Time"; "Dad Wasn't Much for Protocol"; "The Denouement"; "Dr. Einstein Listens To Barbecue Bob's 'Mississippi Heavy Water Blues'"; "Dying Men Prefer Their Privacy"; "Echoes of Ancient Music"; "God Forbid We Disturb the Neighbors"; "The Ground We're Planted In"; "'He Must Mean His Aunt'"; "Henry, Walt, and Bram"; "Horse Sense"; "I Haven't Learned To Love My Solitude"; "Listening to Dylan on the Muni Metro a Month after My Father's Death"; "My Father Lost His Battle with the Lawn"; "No Smoker"; "The Numb Haul"; "A Numbness Where My Wedding Ring Once Was"; "A Parish Church in East Anglia"; "Plague Cemetery, Central London"; "The Poet As Fisherman"; "So Many Deaths"; "Rising Toward Radiance"; "Sturgeon Moon"; "Tear Down the Calendar"; "Through the Window"; "Trout"; "True to His Famous Tag Line"; "The Two Larrys"; "The Vacancy He Leaves"; "We Cannot Risk Love"; "What's Gone Missing"

Hanging Loose: "Answering the Riddle"

Hawai'i Review: "The Unfinished Throne"

Poetry Northwest: "Primer"

Preacher Boy's National Blues Blog: "Dave Van Ronk Was Fond of Tullamore Dew"

The Road Not Taken: "The Journey to Lubeck"; "Watching the December Rain"

Sugar Mule: "Entering the Tomb"

The Tomcat, No. 4: "New World"

On a more personal note, I would like to thank Barry Sheinkopf for once again helping me to bring to fruition this, my fourth book, and for his unflagging support and encouragement over what is now almost forty years. I owe him a debt of gratitude I can never repay. Thanks and acknowledgment are also due to David Gwilym Anthony, Marcus Bales, Barbara Belle-Diamond, Bill Bly, Dan Brady, Barbara Brewer, Buford Buntin, Susan Burke, Diana Caliz, Chris Charles, Peggy Clinton, Bobby Coleman, Robert Crabill, Eric Dahm, Alan Davis, Owen Dunkle, Jack Foley, Hugh Gerstein, Louis Grace, Taylor Graham, Ryan Guth, Tom Hargarten, Johnny Hernandez, Stace Johnson, Jeff Kalmar, Sid Kemp, Ray Kerr, Carrie Knowles, Eugenia Koukounas, Deena Larsen, David Lauter, Vincent Libasci, Kris Lindbeck, April Lindner, April Lindt, Marco Lule, Jeanne Lupton, Gary Mallin, Geraldine McGrath, Tony "Thomas" Mila, Valerie Nance, Mr. Natural, Stephanie Neira, Wendy Overin, Carlos Periañez, Nathan Phelps,

Kathy Reed, Janet Rhodes, Michael Rhodes, Robert-Harry Rovin, Daniel Ryan, Laurie Sato, Sally Love Saunders, Cindy Sawchuck, Marjorie M. Smith, John Strain, John Strain's Room 222 Sixth Period English Class, Linda Tabor-Beck, Janice Tilden, Ken Tray, Sean Tripi, Jeremiah Turner, Ray Valdez, David Van Ausdall, George Van Ausdall, Susan Van Ausdall, Vicki Van Ausdall, Christopher Watkins, Jesse Whitfield, Jennifer Whitten, Socrates Wilde, Stephen Jarrell Williams, Janet Wildung, John Young, and Fritz Zimmerman.

AUTHOR'S NOTE

Sturgeon Moon, my fourth collection of poems, is a work that looks both forward and back. In the most obvious sense, the book, which is dedicated to my late father, the ichthyologist Dr. C. Lavett Smith, chronicles my recollections of him across the years, since many of the poems—especially in the first section, a selection of sonnets—were written about his final days and the ways my life since has been affected by his death.

But in another sense, the book looks forward as well. On June 21, 2017, at the summer solstice, I will turn sixty; this collection is my birthday present to myself. It is new, in that the vast majority of the poems gathered here were written since the publication of my previous collection in 2014. I continue to write almost daily, and the most recent work included here was finished just days before the manuscript was submitted for publication.

A second way in which this present effort looks forward is that it contains the latest installment of a series that I have especially enjoyed writing over the past several years—specifically, humorous narrative poems concerning a character I created, the Reverend Igneous Rock. I said a few years back that I thought the good Reverend and I had journeyed as far together as it seemed we were likely to go; apparently I was mistaken. It now appears that our association may continue for some time yet, and I am willing to follow wherever this boisterous spirit may consent to lead me. Perhaps at some point in the future, I will gather together all of the Igneous Rock poems in a single, definitive omnibus, but I now feel—indeed, I hope—that it may be some while yet before that happens.

That said, *Sturgeon Moon* represents a summing up, also—a handful of the poems, specifically those occupying the second of three free verse sections, are milestones culled from various stages of my "career," such as it has been. With one exception, these earlier poems are old favorites that, for one reason or another, have never previously been included in a book. Some were written as much as forty years ago, when I was a very different person, but I have returned to them because they have continued to resonate with me as decades passed. Welcoming them back into my repertoire after so long is like becoming reacquainted with old friends; I can only hope that they will sit comfortably alongside the more contemporary pieces.

Forty-five years ago, I began my literary life as a rhyming poet, as young people often do. I spent my twenties, thirties, and forties writing almost exclusively free verse, and then, in my early fifties, returned again to rhyme, for a variety of reasons. But if I am a "formalist," I remain a reluctant one. In assembling this collection, I have opted to consign the different kinds of poems to separate sections, rather than mixing forms as I have in the past. The result is, in a manner of speaking, four books in one. It resembles, I can't help but imagine, the early Three Musketeers bars of my parents' recollections, which offered three smaller candy bars of different flavors within a single wrapper. Hopefully, the whole is more than the sum of its parts.

There is one facet of my recent writing that I have deliberately excluded from this volume. My dismay at the outcome of the 2016 presidential election has led me, for the first time ever, to attempt some political poems, with varying degrees of success. These may eventually find a home elsewhere, but, for the moment, they lie beyond the scope of what I aspire to accomplish here.

Robert Lavett Smith,
San Francisco,
January 31, 2017

Table of Contents

The Gentle Dead Draw Near: Sonnets

❄

Sturgeon Moon, 3
No Eulogy Commemorates My Father, 4
The Denouement, 5
The Farthest, 6
My Father Lost His Battle with the Lawn, 7
Every Brown and Withered Winter Lawn, 8
The Numb Haul, 9
In Drenched November, 10
Tear Down the Calendar, 11
Listening to Dylan on the Muni Metro a Month after My Father's Death, 12
December Overtakes Us, 13
Snared, 14
We Cannot Risk Love, 15
A Numbness Where My Wedding Ring Once Was, 16
Beyond the Veil, 17
As If It Mattered Now, 18
No Smoker, 19
At My Father's Deathbed, 20
Dying Men Prefer Their Privacy, 21
Dad Didn't Waste His Time, 22
Dad Wasn't Much for Protocol, 23
Horse Sense, 24
"How about That, Sports Fans?", 25
God Forbid We Disturb the Neighbors, 26
Trout, 27

Could He Have Taken Notes, 28
His Last Wishes, 29
The Fool My Father Sometimes Was, 30
The Vacancy He Leaves, 31
My Father, Near the End, 32
Closure, 33
What's Gone Missing, 34
A Parish Church in East Anglia, 35
Echoes of Ancient Music, 36
A Mean, Unpleasant Guy, 37
Solstice Birthday, 38
"He Must Mean His Aunt", 39
The True Salt of the Earth, 40
The Two Larrys, 41
Grandpa's Campaign in Belgium, 42
Renée Lighting a Cigarette, 43
I Haven't Learned To Love My Solitude, 44
Azure and Indigo, 45
My Shakespeare Student Isn't Showing Up, 46
The Ground We're Planted In, 47
A Faint Combustion in Late Summer Air, 48
These Scribbled Lines Are Disinclined To Rage, 49
Lazarus Rising, 50
I Bet You'd Hate This Poem, 51
A Little Pity Ought To Be Allowed, 52
Our Parents May Be Clinically Insane, 53
Watching the December Rain, 54
A Physical Therapist Volunteers in Port-Au-Prince, 55
A Sort of Mad Salvation, 56
Dr. Einstein Listens to Barbecue Bob's "Mississippi Heavy Water Blues", 57
The Journey to Lubeck, 58

Afterimage, 59
Lonesome Sentinel, 60
The Colossi, 61
Plague Cemetery, Central London, 62
Black and White, 63
My Birth-Blind Eyes Invited Nothing In, 64
Once the Air Clears, 65
Wesley Encounters the Pacific Ocean, 66
Not Getting It, 67
The Dismantled Mansions, 68
Indigenous People's Day, 69
Time To Think about a Taxi, 70
Old Women Wearing Masks, 71
Weather Happens in the Present Tense, 72
True to His Famous Tag Line, 73
The Death of a Beloved Pet, 74
All Saint's Day, 75
The Stricken and the Still, 76
A Grave I've Never Visited, 77
Impatiens, 78
April Fish, 79
Palm Sunday, 80
No Graves Will Open, 81
Your Unfinished Life, 82

The Return of the Reverend Igneous Rock

The Return of the Reverend Igneous Rock, 85
Beulah Rock and the Three-Dollar Turban, 86
The Force Fails To Awaken the Reverend Igneous Rock, 87
Igneous Rock among the Lagomorphs, 89
The Reverend Igneous Rock Mails His Income Tax, 90

The Reverend Igneous Rock Watches It Rain, 91
Igneous Rock and Eustace Tubman, 93
Igneous Rock and the Mermaid, 94
That Professor on TV, 95
How Kumquat Acquired His Moniker, 96
Bunny Ears, 97
Elijah Rock Contemplates Filling His Father's Footsteps, 98
Myrtle Mae Rock Seldom Thinks of the Lord, 99
A Hand-Blown Bottle, 100
Igneous Rock and the Snake Handlers, 101
Igneous Rock Considers Posterity, 102
A Century Ago, 103
Recovering from a Cold, Igneous Rock Unwisely Listens to Blind Willie Johnson, 104
Igneous Rock in the Wee Small Hours, 105
David Bowie, Natalie Cole, and Igneous Rock, 106
Igneous Rock Is No Philosopher, 107
Such Is Fat(e), 108
The Portrait of Lord Jesus, 109
Concerning Angels, 110
Igneous Rock Peruses the Family Album, 111
Igneous Rock Laments the Last Election, 113
Igneous Rock's High School Reunion, 114
A Plain Wooden Cross, 116
Igneous Rock As a Pawn of Memory, 117

The Fallow Heart: Villanelles

Dave Van Ronk Was Fond of Tullamore Dew, 121
A Winter Sky with Ansel Adams Clouds, 122
The Monks of San Durante, 123
The Final Days of These United States, 124

What I Recall Most Vividly Is Silence, 125
The Fallow Heart, 126
A Ghostly Remnant of a House Now Gone, 127
Her Happy Lions, Iced in Red, 128
In Less Than Half a Year I Will Be Sixty, 129
A Silence Fills the Craters of the Tongue, 130
It Will Grow Even Colder Than We Know, 131
The Sculptor's Yard, 132
Your Death Still Feels Immediate Today, 133
Sometimes the Sky Is Pliant, 134
The Cloaked Eroticism of Rose Windows, 135

Curios: Previously Unpublished Poems, 1976–1987

The Wedding, 139
Lullaby and Dirge, 141
Scène de Genre, 143
Apple Trees, 144
New World, 145
Answering the Riddle, 146
Primer, 147
The Peacemakers, 149
Audley End, 150
Hearses, 151
Nocturne, 152
Watching a Blind Man in a Subway Station, 153
Knife Grinder, 154
The Unfinished Throne, 155
The Flower Burning, 156
Dance of the Dresses, 158
If I Had My Druthers, 159

Fickle Weather: Recent Free Verse

A Possible Starting Point, 163
Tastes like Chicken, 164
A Puzzle Box, 165
Decoration Day, 166
Checking, 167
We Can't Be Sure, 168
Death Watch, 169
Cling, If You Must, 170
Rising toward Radiance, 171
Entering the Tomb, 172
The Flames That Claimed Him, 173
My Father's Ashes, 174
L. Frank Baum's Final Words, 175
The Weather Here Doesn't Count for Much, 176
Through the Window, 177
An Old Saw, 178
A Brief Geology of Death, 179
Graffiti, 180
The Last Blacksmith, 181
Walker, 182
Empty Stadium at Night, 183
A Fragment of the Buddha's Skull, 184
Airborne, 185
After the Flood, 186
The Surrealist in Love, 187
Fickle Weather, 188
Henry, Walt, and Bram, 189
The Resonance of Anguish, 190
Concealed, 191
Four Clerihews, 192

The Poet As Fisherman, 193
Seventeen Below, 194
Lying in Bed, 196
Early November Light, 197
Dead Phone Booth, 198
Daybreak in Alabama, 199
A Man Selling Whips on Christmas Eve, 200
Eternity Deepens to Teal, 201
So Many Deaths, 202

The Gentle Dead Draw Near: Sonnets

*"In your mind—in your dreams, in your memories—
sometimes the story begins with the epilogue."*

—John Irving

STURGEON MOON

i.m.: Dr. C. Lavett Smith, 1927–2015

In recent years, the summers have grown colder,
Disturbing in a land besieged by drought.
On the horizon, constellations smolder;
The sturgeon moon seems swollen, hollowed out.
August's long dryness puts late Spring to rout,
And Winter seems eternities away;
Small creatures leave their burrows now, no doubt
Stifled by the insistence of decay.
We understand, of course, you couldn't stay—
Your breathing insubstantial as a wish.
But something intimate returns today,
Beneath this moon we speak of as a fish.
Your body's ash; still somehow you remain,
Beyond the scope of any grief or pain.

NO EULOGY COMMEMORATES MY FATHER

No eulogy commemorates my father,
No wake was held to celebrate his life,
No mourners sought to solace one another,
No sermon gently mocked our disbelief.
My mother—more than sixty years his wife—
Knew his distaste for pomp and circumstance,
His coolly secular approach to grief:
Dad found religion merely an annoyance.
His unembellished exit came to chance;
Old friends were dead already, far away;
Established rituals lacked relevance,
Clichés with nothing meaningful to say.
We'll lay his ashes in the ground again
Some morning when perhaps it will not rain.

THE DENOUEMENT

There is a silence in the grandest music,
A truth withheld in the most brutal poems:
The stillness buried at the core becomes
Presentiment that cuts us to the quick.
We hear it in the gasping of the sick,
The rasp and rattle, pained and tentative,
Of fading life determined still to live,
Tenacity in breath grown low and thick.
Just so, my father reinvents himself.
The fog of his dementia slowly clears;
Memories like volumes on a dusty shelf,
One book whose long-foreshadowed climax nears.
His story—in the end—will write itself,
The denouement perhaps demanding years.

THE FARTHEST

Two months before my father passed away
I spent some time there for the holidays,
Seeing for myself what everybody says:
We cannot reach the dying, try as we may.
Emaciated, tentative and gray,
Dad shuffled through the dull hours in a daze,
Mom's cramped apartment daunting as a maze
Where he invariably lost his way.
The ride to Denver chilled me to the bone,
Hard weather coming, highways brown with snow.
Two hours pinned in a sky like shattered stone;
I called when we made ground in San Francisco.
Dad faltered when Mom handed him the phone:
"And that's the farthest, these days, that you go?"

MY FATHER LOST HIS BATTLE WITH THE LAWN

My father lost his battle with the lawn
Decades before he lost his fight for life—
Crabgrass and gophers gave him no relief,
Though they, by now, like Dad himself, are gone.
This was a war he never could have won,
The thin brown grass a source of constant grief;
Somehow he persevered in his belief
In tender, pliant green, and soldiered on.
His weapon was a push mower from the fifties,
Since he despised the roar and stink of diesel,
And he had no one but himself to please.
He made no headway that I can recall;
And nothing underneath the tulip trees,
In spite of all his labors, changed at all.

EVERY BROWN AND WITHERED WINTER LAWN

i.m.: Dr. C. Lavett Smith, died 2/10/2015

On this first anniversary, I felt
None of the sadness I might have expected—
Perhaps I've kept my heart too well protected,
A fragile fragment swaddled in dark felt.
Patience enough and even glaciers melt;
But I'm the sort who's given to protracted
Pain: endless confrontations reenacted,
Humiliation's resolute assault.
Dad, every brown and withered winter lawn
That will not face the onslaught of your mower
Reminds me forcefully that you are gone.
Green with relief, the grass has won the war;
The daily tonsure you insisted on,
Brutal and pointless, troubles it no more.

THE NUMB HAUL

Rising like souls through dumbly turgid water,
Their always-glassy eyes cold and opaque,
Thousands of glittering bodies coat the lake;
Gill nets await them, poised for silent slaughter.
A carp is ugly once we've stunned and caught her:
Limp in the shocking coil's electric wake,
Grim bounty for formaldehyde to take—
Hardly the graceful angel we once thought her.
Younger, my father wielded that bright coil,
Bottled and labeled each abducted fish,
Charted the artificial lightning's scrawl.
Now, dwindling days drip from his life like oil;
His breath's as insubstantial as a wish,
Succumbing in the end to the numb haul.

IN DRENCHED NOVEMBER

In drenched November, when the mercury
Contracts in every instrument we trust,
Time and hard weather dwindle as they must
Before the season's bleak banality.
The light's a requiem the eye can *see*,
Composed of silences, mist-drizzled dust;
A muted symphony of mold and rust
That wears away our every certainty.
On days like this, the gentle dead draw near,
Although a skeptical, well-ordered mind
Rejects the notion that they may be here.
They keep their secrets; we respond in kind;
Yet something lingers as dull skies grow clear,
Like sodden leaves the dampness leaves behind.

TEAR DOWN THE CALENDAR

i.m.: Dr. C. Lavett Smith, 1927–2015

These are the first months of my father's death.
In Colorado, where he passed away,
The mountains have gone golden with decay;
New snows enclose the summits like a sheath.
Let any elegy we make be brief:
We have already said all one *should* say,
And with the passing of each shrunken day
We grow accustomed to our disbelief.
Abruptly, the autumnal equinox,
When light and darkness reach a stalemate:
And the ash that was his body in a box,
Nothing to argue or negotiate.
Tear down the calendar and stop the clocks?
Meaningless gestures—futile, and too late.

LISTENING TO DYLAN ON THE MUNI METRO A MONTH AFTER MY FATHER'S DEATH

His acid snarl erupts inside my brain,
And suddenly, I'm twenty-two again;
I step across the gap onto the train.
("Oh, *Mama!* Can this really be the N?")
My world still seemed so permanent back then.
This was before I married, lost my wife,
And in the years that followed, many friends—
How innocently sure I was of life!
My father's memory cuts like a knife:
One night he knocked, my music up too loud;
I half expected to be skinned alive,
Certain such ruckus wouldn't be allowed.
To my surprise, Dad grinned and said to me,
"Oh, my. Bob Dylan *is* good, isn't he?"

DECEMBER OVERTAKES US

i.m.: Dr. C. Lavett Smith, 1927–2015

After great loss, the world most often seems
Obscurely lit, as though in monochrome—
Anemic hues are redolent of dreams—
Our briefest journeys lead us far from home.
The days behind weigh more than those to come,
If weight's the word we want for weary light;
The sluggish blood beats its exhausted drum,
And every dusk dims hastily to night.
Perhaps these gnarled scrub pines have it right:
They bend in resignation to the wind,
Their splintered branches broken by the fight,
Teeming green summers long since left behind.
December overtakes us, and we fear
The denouement of this embittered year.

SNARED

i.m.: Dr. C. Lavett Smith, 1927–2015

His chosen science, ichthyology,
Lauded his brilliance, maybe rightly so;
But the advice Dad used to offer me
Was ludicrous, his aphorisms hollow.
The dull-eyed bottom-dwelling carp that go
In lazy circles through the turgid deep
Have learned from birth what little fish must know,
Their lidless stares one short remove from sleep.
But these numb lives leave nothing we need keep:
Snared on the hook of Dad's cold disapproval,
I felt the weight of shame, its reach and sweep—
Something Dad didn't understand at all.
Dispassionate, he managed to survive
Beyond the simple pain of being alive.

WE CANNOT RISK LOVE

"I thought that love would last forever: I was wrong."
—*W. H. Auden*

We cannot risk love without risking loss.
In Northern Colorado months of drought
Have shrunken reservoirs, dried rivers out,
Shorn boulders of their gray array of moss.
The soil hoards its scant moisture, holds it close:
Now, something in the arid light has caught
A nagging absence, lighter than a thought;
Your grief is rather like this, I suppose.
For more than sixty years your lives entwined;
You bore his least idiosyncrasy.
He was not often passionate, but kind—
Though well you knew how stubborn he could be!
His passing leaves deep silences behind,
The price of long familiarity.

A NUMBNESS WHERE MY WEDDING RING ONCE WAS

There is a vacancy on my left hand,
A numbness where my wedding ring once was.
Imagine my third finger wrapped in gauze;
Perhaps you may begin to understand.
Sometimes grief makes a startling demand,
Asserts itself with no apparent cause
So vigorously it must give one pause,
Proclaims the absence of a golden band.
My late wife's death was difficult and slow;
Daily, she sank beneath synaptic sleep.
My father passed not very long ago;
That loss, anticipated, cuts as deep.
Thinking of him, I miss her sorely now—
Miss all the company we cannot keep.

BEYOND THE VEIL

Death's grim finality can't be denied,
Although religions still insist on trying;
The awful truth is all of us are dying,
Caught in oblivion's onrushing tide.
There may be nothing on the other side:
A starless river weary of its flowing;
A bitter wind; a distant tempest brewing—
It probably won't matter once I've died.
But I remember having asked my Dad
What waited for us all beyond the veil.
He weighed the question carefully, then said,
"When we observe the mind begin to fail,
It's nothing but brain function going bad—
That's not what the brain *does*; no, not at all."

AS IF IT MATTERED NOW

My father, in his final days of life,
Had difficulty lying for long in bed—
I seriously doubt he could have said
What gnawed his failing nerves beyond relief.
Too terminal to face the surgeon's knife,
He acquiesced to ultrasound instead;
Since everybody knew he'd soon be dead,
Treatments were pointless, destined to be brief.
A shapeless shadow in his lower back,
The scans suggested, *could* be cancerous,
Or just an errant phantom, some feedback
Defective scanners have been known to cause.
Benign, malignant—it's gone up in smoke—
I still can't help but wonder what it was.

NO SMOKER

Dad wasn't ever what you'd call a smoker:
He managed one cigar in fifteen years,
A fragrant pipe some evenings after dinner—
So rarely that it caught us unawares.
But as the haze around his passing clears,
I find myself besieged by memory:
A pungent sweetness wafting down the stairs
That both repelled and fascinated me.
How strangely lucid these olfactory
Impressions seeping from my childhood:
The slow combustion of dried leaves like tea,
Like incense, or like gently seasoned wood:
The ghostly resonance of fresh tobacco
Up in his study, fifty years ago.

AT MY FATHER'S DEATHBED

"You mean you haven't told him that he's *dying?*
Then what the hell's he think he's in here for?"
My mother bites her lip without replying,
Having endured such foolishness before.
The hospice nurse prates on, oblivious,
Blundering through a painful situation.
What's the appropriate response to this?
Smoldering silence? Outraged indignation?
What Dad must think, it's difficult to say—
He's unresponsive now to anything;
His eyes are tightly sealed since yesterday;
He's quiet, save for ragged, shallow breathing.
This time tomorrow evening he'll be dead:
Wry witticisms, sadly, left unsaid.

DYING MEN PREFER THEIR PRIVACY

Dying men prefer their privacy, we say,
Most often passing quietly, alone—
The hospice nurse on duty called away,
All the exhausted relatives gone home.
A thin electric scribble in the gloom,
The monitor inscribed Dad's final hours;
He sank beneath the stillness in the room,
With no companions save a few cold stars.
His death, just after nine, was never ours;
Something to be remembered, but not shared;
Like an illusionist who disappears,
His exit had already been prepared.
As though it were expected courtesy,
He slipped away with no one there to see.

DAD DIDN'T WASTE HIS TIME

He'd leave a blowfish rotting in a drawer,
Answer our home phone "Ichthyology,"
Give quaint ideas his imprimatur,
Quite unaware of their absurdity.
A champion of impracticality,
Dad didn't waste his time on social graces;
Safe in the bubble of his certainty,
He flourished in the most exotic places.
The irony I must begin to face is
I *did* learn something from him after all:
He chose to leave me to my own devices,
Knowing I'd have to learn to fly, or fall;
He spread his love of learning by example,
Leading a life both generous and full.

DAD WASN'T MUCH FOR PROTOCOL

As curator of Ichthyology,
Dad sometimes found himself in the position
To welcome visitors of some distinction—
And, in at least one instance, royalty.
This is the incident a friend related:
Apparently the Crown Prince of Japan,
Who spoke no English, was a tiny man
Whose majesty Dad quietly deflated.
Arriving with a bevy of attendants,
He stood among the jars of pickled fish
Attired in a splendid purple sash,
The very soul of pomp and circumstance.
The story goes that Dad addressed him thus:
"I'm honored to have met Your Royal Minus."

HORSE SENSE

Dad's fatherly advice was *always* wrong.
Raised on a dairy farm in New York State,
He never managed to anticipate
Trouble, hocking his horse sense for a song.
The safest bet was just to play along—
His harebrained schemes weren't open to debate,
And I learned early not to take the bait:
Decades of stifled laughter make one strong.
I had to draw the line at his insistence,
When I was struggling as a book store clerk,
I sacrifice my weekend on the chance
The boss was grateful for my unpaid work—
A doubtful move in any circumstance.
I loved my Dad, but he could be a jerk.

"HOW ABOUT THAT, SPORTS FANS?"

Why my late father—himself no sports fan—
Latched on to that athletic turn of phrase
Is something that continues to amaze
Me; Dad was sometimes a peculiar man.
Explain his fascination, if you can,
With an expression scorned in bygone days
As being among the cheapest of clichés
Decades before it reached ESPN.
Dad hardly ever cottoned to surprise,
Hoping to cultivate a suave impression;
Life's harshness remained hidden from his eyes.
He never quite outgrew the Great Depression
And, when the unexpected did arise,
Possessed no expletives he could rely on.

GOD FORBID WE DISTURB THE NEIGHBORS

Our Cape Cod in New Jersey was the showpiece
For the development, when it was built—
This meant we had a spacious yard with trees,
A creek that was, in summer, mostly silt.
It meant the nearby houses were more distant
Than usual in that bland suburban sprawl,
And I have little doubt it also meant
The neighbors barely heard us, if at all.
But every morning at five forty-four,
One minute before my alarm clock rang,
My father nearly battered down my door,
And launched into his matinal harangue.
Had I not silenced it at once, I fear
The consequences would have been severe.

TROUT

The way my father used to gut a fish?
More ichthyologist than fisherman—
Such surgical precision sometimes can
Leave an incision bloodless as a wish.
My life was tepid, like a petri dish,
Faults splayed as if in a dissecting pan:
My gait, my weight, my not yet being a man,
My in-turned toes when I was seven-ish.
Dad split the trout he caught from snout to tail,
Arranged their organs on the weathered dock:
The lobed gray brain, the threaded purple trail
Of gonads, lidless eyes still glazed with shock.
The breathless fish, convulsed, would splash and flail,
Dad's disapproval steady as a rock.

COULD HE HAVE TAKEN NOTES

i.m.: Dr. C. Lavett Smith, 1927–2015

Believe, if you insist, in the Beyond:
Heavenly cities built on metaphor
Are poor attempts to posit something more,
A desperate tactic of the moribund.
My Dad was a reluctant Protestant,
Raised Methodist because his mother was;
I doubt the holy ever gave him pause;
The natural world was his one sacrament.
The night he died—although I wasn't there—
I'm sure he must have been intrigued by death,
Inquisitive right to his final breath,
For Dad found points of interest everywhere.
Could he have taken notes, he would have done—
Until the very instant he was gone.

HIS LAST WISHES

Hamburg, New York, where my late Dad was raised,
Skirted the leaden vastness of Lake Erie—
Too far ashore to navigate its dreary
Expanse, he felt its presence all his days.
And I don't care what anybody says:
The oily reaches of that inland sea
Called to the farmer he would never be,
Moved him to curiosity, to praise.
Now, nearly ninety years have come and gone;
All that remains of Dad: a box of ashes,
Some research friends will doubtless carry on.
But if we seek to honor his last wishes,
Someday when Mom is also dust, someone
Will bring him home to his beloved fishes.

THE FOOL MY FATHER SOMETIMES WAS

I bless the fool my father sometimes was;
I bless as well the sophist he could be;
His mind embraced and valued equally
The truly brilliant, the preposterous.
I never saw him angry without cause
But have to laugh at the absurdity
Of such a stubborn eccentricity:
Life's contradictions seldom gave him pause.
I will not picture him, in years to come,
As the gaunt phantom of his final days,
Nor as the stranger we must each become
As feelings falter and the mind decays—
He wore his certainties with such aplomb,
Even his faults deserve my grudging praise.

THE VACANCY HE LEAVES

Back in the early seventies, my father
Remained submerged completely, weeks on end,
Researching, cooking, sleeping underwater,
Sharing cramped quarters with his closest friend.
The habitats were primitive at best;
One had been salvaged from a storage tank;
But I recall being very much impressed,
Although these sunken labs were small and dank.
Once, at a base camp in the Virgin Islands,
I scrutinized the point Dad should emerge:
A distance no child truly understands
Scarred the bright tide, anxiety writ large.
Today, in death, the vacancy he leaves
Encompasses that void beneath the waves.

MY FATHER, NEAR THE END

The aging brain, sheathed in its dome of bone,
Weighs two or three pounds at the uttermost,
And yet its convolutions have played host
To countless displaced wanderers, now gone.
My father, near the end, was surely one;
His brilliant scientific mind was lost
To what became a casual holocaust—
The slow encroachment of oblivion.
The tallow of the neurons burning low,
There comes a final, agonizing thirst;
Then, even the dispassionate allow
Age and infirmity have done their worst.
The highways of his mind are empty now,
The broken legions of his blood, dispersed.

CLOSURE

Unable to unburden one another,
They gathered at his side the night Dad passed,
While I was firmly told I needn't bother
Booking a flight once he had breathed his last.
The granite sky is somber, overcast:
Vague shadows blur, suggesting poor exposure,
As though the present can't suppress the past—
The atmosphere itself deprived of closure.
I know already all I need to know, sure
My absence from the deathbed didn't matter;
There was no comfort offered, and no censure;
It would have made no difference if there were.
Abruptly, this grim weather overhead
Snaps shut above me like a dark eyelid.

WHAT'S GONE MISSING

On a late summer evening such as this—
Deep in September, when the weather's warm—
One sometimes feels inclined to reminisce
About the times before life meant us harm.
There's no cause for immediate alarm;
We've grown inured to loss in recent years;
But reassurances that would disarm
Increasingly must bow to strange new fears.
And just at sunset, something disappears
Along with the last remnants of the day—
Dead constellations glitter far and fierce—
Precisely what's gone missing we can't say.
We cannot help but shiver at such moments,
Though ours is not an age inclined to omens.

A PARISH CHURCH IN EAST ANGLIA

Summer, 1982

Against the splendor of the rose window,
The spectrum shatters into varied hues,
Light's burning sternness finally diffuse:
Divinity draws near enough to know.
The shadowed sanctuary is aglow;
Old varnish blazes on abandoned pews
That living worshipers no longer use,
Their brazen nameplates darkened long ago.
Decades from now, when I'm abruptly old,
I'll pray, perhaps, in a more sterile setting—
Carpets in lieu of flagstones, no damp cold,
The mildew put to rout by central heating.
My spirit will refuse to be consoled,
Though I may not recall what I'm regretting.

ECHOES OF ANCIENT MUSIC

i.m.: Galway Kinnell, 1927–2014

Your voice was resonant and gently wise,
More penetrating than perhaps we knew.
A passion for the craft preceded you:
So did the patient kindness in your eyes.
As starlings, when they catch an updraft, rise,
Whispering wing beats lifted into blue,
Something you often told our class rings true,
Hoisting my hurt heart upward to clear skies.
You said that we write poetry because
We hear an ancient music in its lines,
That otherwise we'd all be writing prose.
Our scansion betrays raggedness at times
Whose implications only the blood knows;
You offered us a taste of the sublime.

A MEAN, UNPLEASANT GUY

Bill Lester was a mean, unpleasant guy,
A copy editor for Prentice Hall.
Thirty years on, I vividly recall
His hard, pinched features, cold judgmental eye.
Freelance proofreaders function on the fly—
With luck I barely dealt with Bill at all—
His mind, like his cramped cubicle, was small;
I'd grab the galleys, bid a quick goodbye.
"Yes, dear; we'll have him over, if we must...
No, I can't promise, but I'll look at it. . . ."
(His frown made clear whatever they'd discussed
He'd had it up to here with her bullshit.)
Then, slamming down the phone in blunt disgust,
Bill sneered, "Oh God! I hope you're not a *poet!*"

SOLSTICE BIRTHDAY

"Yesterday it was my birthday;
I hung one more year on the line."
—Paul Simon

The dim days past, light lengthens into light,
For now at least, and in the cyclic sense—
But I turn sixty less than one year hence,
So much undone, so much I can't unwrite.
I've tried to nurture love, but haven't, quite:
The weight of disappointment seems immense,
And in my neighborhood the dark is dense;
The stars stay hidden on the clearest night.
Still, yesterday brought much to celebrate:
An unaccustomed sweetness in the wine;
Moments of candor to appreciate;
Failures accepted gracefully as mine.
For some time yet, the light will linger late
As strands of burnished brightness intertwine.

"HE MUST MEAN HIS AUNT"

A letter from the French exchange student
Who lived with them in Laurie's Senior year
Irritates Mom, who simply will not hear
My careful explanation of its content.
He's staying, he writes, with Uncle Jean Marie,
A man I visited while overseas.
The first name's "John"; the second, meant to please
The Virgin, in that very Catholic country.
"He has to mean his *aunt*," my Mom insists,
Convinced a mistranslation is to blame;
Once I've explained the nature of the name,
Her trademark stubbornness—of course—persists.
She either will not change her mind, or can't,
Repeating firmly, "He must mean his aunt."

THE TRUE SALT OF THE EARTH

A trailer park near Cleveland, May, 1980

My cousins were, my mother staunchly claimed,
Ordinary folks, the true salt of the earth.
I struggled to forgive—for what it's worth—
Their outworn attitudes, but felt ashamed.
Small-town Ohioans cannot be blamed,
Perhaps, for that sad accident of birth;
They gave the unfamiliar a wide berth;
The slightest quirk was readily defamed.
One case in point: a family picnic. What
I overheard would scarcely reassure
Me, or help to persuade me they were not
The narrow bigots I so feared they were:
"We think we may have seen a *Jew* once, but
Since it was from a distance, we're not sure."

THE TWO LARRYS

My mother's much too stubborn to have learned
A foreign language, since the native speakers—
Whose accents have the gall to challenge hers—
Are simply wrong, as far as she's concerned.
A case in point's the afternoon in Paris
When we were headed for the Tuileries
And she nagged passers-by incessantly
For directions to what *she* called "The Two Larrys."
All her entreaties met with frank confusion,
And Mom, who's always played by her own rules,
Concluding that the French were simply fools,
Somehow escaped the obvious conclusion.
She found the gardens and adjacent palace
Purely by chance and not by skill, alas.

GRANDPA'S CAMPAIGN IN BELGIUM

Grandfather Smith survived the First World War,
Returning to his dairy farm upstate;
Though doubtless haunted by the hell he saw,
He never mentioned it, resigned to fate.
My father, christened with his father's name,
Replaced a nameless, stillborn, older brother;
In the late twenties Dad was right on time—
Too young for one war, too old for another.
Had Vietnam grown uglier or stranger,
I might have found myself compelled to serve;
Cerebral palsy kept me out of danger,
A grim reprieve I seemed not to deserve.
Grandpa's campaign in Belgium must suffice;
No son of mine will fuel the sacrifice.

RENÉE LIGHTING A CIGARETTE

Renée was Black, spectacularly fat—
In short, my absolutely perfect woman.
My lust for her was almost superhuman;
She always seemed a bit bemused by that.
And every time she lit a cigarette
I watched in fascination, a non-smoker
For whom her habit only served to mold her
The more exotic, harder to forget.
On Mission Street she'd cup her hands around
A flaring match to shield it from the wind;
I loved the glow it bathed her features in;
Igniting flame made such a sexy sound.
Then, when she exhaled, rags of smoke uncurled
Through streetlight beams—each shining thread, a world.

I HAVEN'T LEARNED TO LOVE MY SOLITUDE

"O, que j'aime la solitude!"
—Marc-Antoine Girard de Saint-Amant (1594–1661)

One Marc-Antoine Girard de Saint-Amant
Praised places he called "sacred to the night,"
Far from the city's stale, degraded light:
Festering marshlands, ruined battlements.
I know the holy quietude he meant;
Enraptured by his lines, I tried to write
An eloquent adieu to all things bright,
But I was much too young, my time misspent.
I haven't learned to love my solitude.
The dull dead throng around me every day:
I know the scent of almonds they exude,
The gentle resignation of decay.
I know they come to comfort, not to brood—
I also know they haven't come to stay.

AZURE AND INDIGO

The brownie was particularly strong—
Perception left reality behind
While opening strange portals in my mind,
Visions too vivid to endure for long.
Sad troubadours once sang in Aquitaine
Of brutal panoramas like this view
Woven entirely in shades of blue:
Azure and indigo, aquamarine.
The tapestry, in spots, was worn away;
The warp and woof consumed by moths and time;
But armored men and chargers reigned sublime,
Trappings, each gruesome detail of the fray.
Yet this unearthly *Gobelins* had to be
Hallucination, and not memory.

MY SHAKESPEARE STUDENT ISN'T SHOWING UP

The Prince of Denmark and his ghostly dad
Exchange their windy ramparts for a classroom;
This new millennium is not half bad,
Although it also has its share of gloom.
My Shakespeare student isn't showing up,
And dreary Hamlet's hungry now, and bored.
He grimaces at his phantasmal Pop
And fidgets. Neither of them says a word.
I don't know what to tell them. After all,
The kid likes reading, chose the play himself.
Nine pages in, with kingdoms poised to fall,
We're three sad sacks discarded on the shelf.
A little courtesy is all we want;
Now lunchtime's almost over. *Exeunt.*

THE GROUND WE'RE PLANTED IN

For Jennifer E. Whitten's birthday, September 18, 2015

As we grow older, so our roots grow deeper:
Like steadfast trees accustomed to strong wind
We come to trust the ground we're planted in,
The way a dream must learn to trust the sleeper.
Not every summer evening is a "keeper":
Consulting cloudless midnight skies we find
Familiar constellations realigned,
Our fortunes other than we hoped they were.
And yet, the leaves reciting overhead
Know the redemptive strength of poetry—
We relish their green cadences instead
Of stones and sorrows stirring restlessly.
Fireflies frolic on the road ahead;
We are already where we need to be.

A FAINT COMBUSTION IN LATE SUMMER AIR

For the fifteenth anniversary.

Though death encompasses us, we ignore it,
A faint combustion in late summer air—
But at the instant when the first plane hit,
Its force was palpable, felt everywhere.
Despite nostalgia that detains me there,
I woke to placid California light,
Far from a smoky dawn beyond repair,
To foliage both innocent and bright.
Woke to a silence waiting to ignite:
Grief flakes like ashes from contorted walls
Whose image, pixelated on the night,
Only solidifies as darkness falls.
That silence goes on ringing in our ears,
Still undiminished after fifteen years.

THESE SCRIBBLED LINES ARE DISINCLINED TO RAGE

> *"Police killed at least 102 unarmed black people in 2015, nearly twice each week."*
>
> *—Mappingpoliceviolence.org*

My late wife Pat, herself a woman of color,
Was gentle and dependably humane,
Able to empathize with others' pain—
"The mate that fate had me created for."
There's no doubt she would openly deplore
Such wanton violence. Today, again,
I read online about unarmed Black men
Gunned down, too numbed to easily keep score.
These scribbled lines are disinclined to rage;
I champion the maimed beauty of the world:
But lately, every moment tests our courage.
Midsummer skies, fierce eyes, burn blue and cold,
Lit by a fear no love would dare assuage.
Nothing remains for me to have or hold.

LAZARUS RISING

"And he that was dead came forth, bound hand and foot with graveclothes."
—John 11:44

The cold that seemed to smolder in his bones
Diminishes at last; the sluggish blood,
Acquainted with the stubbornness of stones,
Begins to stir, dull arteries to flood.
Lungs that once rattled, dry as firewood,
Abruptly clear, and swell with hopeful breath;
His life's his own again—that's understood—
No longer held in thrall to cheated Death.
But he seems troubled by his time beneath
The layered clay, in realms of rotting mold:
Although his sojourn underground was brief,
He pines for darkness, cannot be consoled.
The years ahead will find him ill at ease,
Consumed by grim eventualities.

I BET YOU'D HATE THIS POEM

i.m.: Franz Wright, 1953–2015

I bet you'd hate the fact this is a sonnet,
Preferring jagged lines imbued with silence,
Words that don't hesitate to do us violence
And won't play all the cards they hold just yet.
Forget about a strict pentameter,
A bland anachronism with no future—
Better the lyricism of a suture,
The studied elegance of a skull fracture,
The horrid beauty of a stifled cry
That resonates with stunned and speechless pain.
Beyond the pillaged corn at dusk, warm rain
Spits broken lightning from a hemorrhaged sky;
A few cold stars try stubbornly to rise,
The new moon like a coin for your dead eyes.

A LITTLE PITY OUGHT TO BE ALLOWED

For what would have been our 18th wedding anniversary.

Some days the emptiness is palpable,
The vacancy that haunts the heart of things—
A churchyard cherub's broken limestone wings,
The stumbling twilight that seems poised to fall.
The worst of it is that you still recall
Thin summer skies whose silken shimmerings,
As if in answer to your deepest yearnings,
Proffered the Future like a siren call.
But in November, when the rotting moon's
Pinned to a night that stifles like a shroud,
We see our callow dreams reduced to ruins.
A little pity ought to be allowed,
Nostalgia for those sentimental tunes.

OUR PARENTS MAY BE CLINICALLY INSANE

Perhaps it's symptomatic of their age.
More obviously than in former years,
Our ailing parents, as the darkness nears,
Regard life through accumulated rage.
The mind, allowed to languish, is a cage,
A prison even as it disappears,
A storage closet full of hoarded fears,
An ill-lit backdrop for an empty stage.
It's *possible* they're clinically insane,
Something no one is likely to admit.
Deep in the furrows of an aging brain,
Deformed and ludicrous ideas sit.
While moments of lucidity remain,
What can we do but make the best of it?

WATCHING THE DECEMBER RAIN

Here, in this climate where there is no snow,
Gunmetal skies sob like a rag wrung out;
Precipitation brings relief from drought,
But something in the weather lays me low.
I started dreading Christmas years ago:
A season not of faith, but nagging doubt,
Gifting no miracles to sing about,
No plausible salvation that I know.
Heaven's neglected, an outworn conceit;
The season's neither sacred nor profane,
Its promises withdraw on plodding feet.
So I stand watching the December rain,
A weak gray drizzle sizzling on concrete,
A damp hosanna in a rusty drain.

A PHYSICAL THERAPIST VOLUNTEERS IN PORT-AU-PRINCE

The man has injured his back in a fall.
—So, what have you been doing for the pain?
—I drink a draught of goat's blood mixed with gall;
I pray a lot; wait for the moon to wane.
—And has this helped? (He grins; of course it has.)
—I leave a mango by my door at night
In case a hungry poltergeist should pass,
And bathe in holy water by candlelight.
—Let me suggest some other remedies.
These leg lifts I'm about to demonstrate
Should, if you do them daily, help to ease
Lumbar constrictions as you shift your weight.
The patient frowns, his weathered face like wood.
—That *nonsense* will not do me any good.

A SORT OF MAD SALVATION

A Coptic icon somehow come to life,
He strides the sparsely planted median,
His wooden cross thrust forward like a knife—
A minor codicil in God's Grand Plan.
I guess you've got to hand it to the man;
His shouted words and weird gesticulation,
Outroaring passing bus or minivan,
Prove more than equal to the situation.
The tangled beard is part of the equation,
As is the long black cassock that he wears;
It seems as though a sort of mad salvation
Has caught the drowsy traffic unawares.
And the declining sun seems poised to hold
His fervor on a field of beaten gold.

DR. EINSTEIN LISTENS TO BARBECUE BOB'S "MISSISSIPPI HEAVY WATER BLUES"

For Christopher Watkins

Late nights, he sets aside his violin,
Relaxes—as a rule—to classical.
Quite honestly, he simply can't recall
Who gave him this old acetate, or when.
The needle drops and the blue notes begin.
It's nothing he's familiar with at all:
Like stillness deepening before a squall,
That brooding instant a hard rain blows in.
"The Mississippi Heavy Water Blues,"
Grimly coincidental name aside,
Gives the professor nothing he can use;
He still prefers deuterium oxide.
In what weird universe will he cut loose,
Put down his rosined bow, take up the slide?

THE JOURNEY TO LUBECK

Young J. S. Bach, it's known, traversed deep snow,
Drawn by reports of Buxtehude's playing.
When silence fell again, he rose to go;
Finding himself entranced, he wound up staying.
Today, raised on recordings, we forget
How rare a pleasure it must once have been
To hear a rondeau or a minuet
Performed by virtuosi seldom seen.
High in the organ loft, thick, clustered chords
Must have seemed palpable enough to hold;
Today, no digital podcast affords
Encounters so immediate, so bold—
As stunning as a windswept coast might be
To someone who had never seen the sea.

AFTERIMAGE

Already your surrender is beginning:
At dawn, the ragged clouds are distant, cold;
The daily massacre starts to unfold—
A pointless struggle you despair of winning.
The planet, sickened by its constant spinning,
Knows in its stony bones it's growing old,
As you know too, not needing to be told;
Your hair is colorless, distinctly thinning.
A cherished portrait in a shabby frame
Watches benignly from a nearby wall:
An afterimage, oft-entreated name.
Ten empty years with no relief at all;
Everything different, somehow the same;
The usual morning noises far and small.

LONESOME SENTINEL

Glimpsed through the tinted window of a bus
On the New Jersey Turnpike at twilight
A broken smokestack pressed against the night
Proclaimed the place a vanished factory was.
The lip was crumbled, but the stack stood tall:
A pedestal supporting the first stars,
Rising above the flood of passing cars;
A derelict, a lonesome sentinel.
When I was younger, and still lived Back East,
I watched each evening for this one landmark
As the surrounding neighborhood grew dark;
It must be thirty years by now, at least.
Why did this simple thing impress me so?
Well, for the life of me, I still don't know.

THE COLOSSI

Grain elevators dwarf Midwestern towns
The way the great cathedrals dwarf old cities
Through whose dark lanes the Angelus resounds
Like nothing in this country—more's the pity.
But there *is* something holy in such places,
Especially those abandoned since the War;
Dorothea Lange immortalized grim faces
Afraid of what tomorrow held in store:
The sunburnt seraphim of the new order
Eking subsistence from a famished land,
A barren waste of dust and squalid water
Above which the colossi made their stand
Like emptied temples to some vast defeat,
Casting long shadows on the dead main street.

PLAGUE CEMETERY, CENTRAL LONDON

Unearthed March 11, 2015

The stubborn earth reluctantly discloses
A holocaust all decency disowns:
Strewn liberally among these blackened bones,
We find the withered stems of ancient roses.
The simplest explanation, we suppose, is
The scent of petals—not so much a cure
As meant to mask a stinking, putrid sore—
A palliative to soothe medieval noses.
Here, several hundred of these ill-starred dead
Lie helter-skelter in a common grave,
The last rites very likely left unsaid
For souls the Church was powerless to save.
They turned from Heaven, seeking death instead,
The one salvation they could still believe.

BLACK AND WHITE

My fifth grade teacher, back in the late sixties,
Would watch *Divorce Court* every day at recess.
His marriage then was on the skids, I guess;
As kids, we barely noticed things like these.
Those tiny, cheesy, black and white TVs
Were seldom used for very much at school—
Every Apollo moon shot, as a rule;
Newscasts, perhaps, in rare emergencies.
The image flickered, and the sound was poor—
We counted down in unison from ten—
We'd one day ride that rocket, to be sure.
Just thinking of it puts me there again:
Forgotten classmates gathered on the floor,
All waiting for The Future to begin.

MY BIRTH-BLIND EYES INVITED NOTHING IN

In nineteen fifty-seven, I would arrive
Just after midnight on the summer solstice,
The hapless victim of divine injustice:
Born early, and at first, barely alive.
My birth-blind eyes invited nothing in.
In the glass coffin of the incubator,
One of so many tombs life had in store,
I struggled fiercely with a fierce season.
Later, when light began to penetrate
That gentle darkness stolen from the womb,
Phantasmal figures hovered in the room:
Something unspeakable was lying in wait.
A lifetime's worth of trying would not dispel
A radiance that didn't wish me well.

ONCE THE AIR CLEARS

When Dylan Thomas drank at the White Horse,
The world awoke to grainy black and white;
There was the menace of the Bomb, of course,
And sputnik roamed the anxious skies at night.
Our parents' generation never quite
Outgrew the paranoia of those years—
Progress dissolves in psychedelic light,
A pleasant dream that quickly disappears.
So now we're steeped in shit up to our ears.
I wish there were a chance this might end well,
But we may find ourselves, once the air clears,
Tenants in some new rung of Dante's Hell:
Despondent shades assembled decades hence,
Still stubbornly protesting innocence.

WESLEY ENCOUNTERS THE PACIFIC OCEAN

At fourteen, Wesley very seldom speaks—
His reticence is typical of autism,
Though what concealed trauma struck him dumb
Has been the subject of debate for weeks.
Befriended by both gutter punks and geeks,
This lanky, vaguely likable Chinese,
Who seems determined in his way to please,
Waits calmly for a dawn that never breaks.
A shining revelation of this calm,
Water elicits his profound devotion:
An outing at the beach should be most welcome.
Eyes filled with something deeper than emotion,
Stunned, rooted ankle-deep in surging foam,
Wesley encounters the Pacific Ocean.

NOT GETTING IT

A favorite student maybe best left nameless,
His graciousness perhaps a bit askew,
Does unto others as he'd have them do,
And just can't fathom history's nastiness.
I'm grateful for such innocence, I guess—
His guileless manner often gets me through
On days when nothing else in life rings true,
And, usually, his quirkiness seems harmless.
But after class today he came to me
And I was frankly stunned by what he said—
A whispered plea for beauty amidst squalor,
Offered with absolute sincerity:
"Why couldn't the S. S. at least have painted
The Auschwitz barracks in some cheerful colors?"

THE DISMANTLED MANSIONS

i.m.: Patricia Lewis Smith, 1953–2005

You were a quietly observant Christian
Never inclined to proselytize or scold,
But very much a member of the fold
Who made it clear you *did* believe in Heaven.
A loving Savior would have let you in;
Bereaved, and desperate to be consoled
By reassuring platitudes we're sold,
I soon grew ill at ease in borrowed skin.
If not the Citadel you'd hoped to see—
Which I'm inclined to think was never there—
You've reached a plausible facsimile
As incandescent ash adrift somewhere,
Already thinning into piety
In the dismantled mansions of the air.

INDIGENOUS PEOPLE'S DAY

As everybody knows—but few admit—
No one's *indigenous* to anywhere;
Even the native nations planted here
Descend from distant nomads older yet.
And what is home, but somewhere we forget?
Pigments and eyes can lie; in all our hair
Are twined the torrid sun, the arctic air:
Traces of Tanzania or Tibet.
Columbus brought disease and misery
To cultures with no need to be "discovered,"
Smudging our convoluted history—
A bloodbath from which nothing was recovered.
The daughter I might well have had haunts me:
Her amber skin, her ice-gray gaze that hovers.

TIME TO THINK ABOUT A TAXI

It may be time to think about a taxi.
The homeless man who stood to let me sit
Hissed, "Mister, all you had to do was ax me,"
Then spent the next ten minutes talking shit.
Apparently the driver was afraid
To simply throw the asshole off the bus;
He made no comment, staring straight ahead,
Clearly offended like the rest of us.
The gaunt, unshaven zombie next to me,
Ragged and filthy, bloodshot eyes glazed over,
Let loose a torrent of obscenity
From which the sunrise never did recover.
Insouciant, bright yellow cabs sped by,
Beneath the dome of flushed, embarrassed sky.

OLD WOMEN WEARING MASKS

Some passengers, especially the Chinese,
Don surgical masks when they ride the bus—
Whether from a germ phobic fear of us
Or intimate acquaintance with disease.
They've infiltrated every part of town,
Elderly women with quick, frightened eyes
That register a sort of shocked surprise
Even as their strange garb conceals a frown.
They call to mind those blue-veiled Tuareg traders,
Grim nomads robed in vivid indigo:
But these are Cantonese grandmothers who
Regard the unfamiliar as a curse,
Venturing forth to market so they can
Purchase a newly ripened durian.

WEATHER HAPPENS IN THE PRESENT TENSE

Indian summer infiltrates the Bay,
Quite unexpectedly, in late September:
Worn skies a uniform metallic gray
Whose dullness no one chooses to remember.
The setting sun has dwindled to an ember,
And still the air is stifling, close and dense;
Well, other evenings on the East Coast were
Far worse than this, in my experience.
But weather happens in the present tense:
The silence settles in here like dry rot,
A victim beyond reach of recompense
Desperate to pass for something it is not.
Give me Manhattan asphalt soft with heat—
The kind that blisters our unwary feet.

TRUE TO HIS FAMOUS TAG LINE

i.m.: Leonard Nimoy, died February 27, 2015

He passed at 83, leaving no doubt,
True to his famous tag line, he'd lived long;
Forty-two million net or thereabout
Suggest he also prospered—am I wrong?
His lungs were ruined, but his spirit, strong:
He played a character without emotion
So passionately we were swept along,
Offering him our unreserved devotion.
His death evokes Newton's first law of motion:
He's left us, but continues on his way;
The loss unsettles us like an explosion;
Perhaps we'll meet him in the stars someday.
For now this vanished icon of our youth
Still speaks with vision, clarity, and truth.

THE DEATH OF A BELOVED PET

i.m.: Gracie Sato, c.1994–2016

The death of a beloved pet—a cat—
Cuts just as deep as any human death:
An absence numbs the blood, invades the breath,
The moment moans *in pace requiescat.*
Some bonds are only rarely hinted at;
The many facets of the feline life
Are all built on unquestioning belief
In total love. What human offers *that?*
Wide eyes ignite, metallic in the dark,
Scanning her dreaming mistress like twin moons;
Companionship has been her heart's whole work.
Even at twenty-two, she's gone too soon—
Gracie, whose calm contentment lit the spark,
Her easy rumble, sadly also gone.

ALL SAINT'S DAY

November is an unforgiving time;
The cold air wounds us with its clarity;
Nature denuded, like exacting rhyme,
Lays bare its primitive severity.
As autumn dies, it's difficult to be
Sanguine concerning seasons yet to come;
The tattered light's essential poverty
Paints even the most hopeful life lonesome.
The wind that stirs bare branches is struck dumb:
Sounds carry farther, but there is no sound;
Our blood is sluggish, beats a muted drum;
Our doubts are both persistent and profound.
No saint I know would deign to bless this day,
This sky like tarnished silver, hard and gray.

THE STRICKEN AND THE STILL

i.m.: R. S. Thomas, 1913–2000

The poet photographed deplorably—
A stern old codger, country clergyman,
Stubbornly Welsh and fiercely Anglican—
In every portrait he scowls bitterly.
Oh, how he raged against modernity!
Refrigerators were decried in sermons;
Machines he saw as little more than vermin,
Distractions from our spirituality.
But the harsh music of the balding hills
Flowed freely, unencumbered, in his lines:
He caught the cadence of the health, the ills,
Of those who tilled the earth or delved the mines.
He moved among the stricken and the still,
Attuned to more celestial designs.

A GRAVE I'VE NEVER VISITED

i.m.: Adrienne Stengel, 1958–2006

Only two photographs turn up online:
Your face, calm and unwrinkled, is the same,
Your gentle grace, so daunting to define;
A granite marker bears your maiden name.
The stone, elaborate, is fashioned in
The image of the temple at Wilmette,
Another journey missed I don't regret—
There are some wars no heart can ever win.
"Enable this bird trainèd by thy hand
To soar in the eternal rose garden,"
Reads the inscription there, and once again
I feel the faith I could not understand.
Somewhere, perhaps, you cherish your belief;
All these years later, I'm left only grief.

IMPATIENS

i.m.: Adrienne Stengel, 1958–2006

Pink, heart-shaped petals, vivid in soft light,
Reduced to nothing now but memory,
Still stain a letter I will never write,
Dead words encrusted with futility.
A casual gift bestowed in nineteen-eighty,
This common plant became a metaphor
For all the girls determined not to love me,
Warning of what my life might hold in store.
It simply doesn't matter anymore:
That old acquaintance that I used to know,
Destined to be a friend and nothing more,
Succumbed to cancer several years ago.
Time would suffice to pull it all apart—
Each blossom like a fragile, pliant heart.

APRIL FISH

Poisson d'avril—as they would say in France—
Or "April fish," whatever *that* may mean.
(Medieval custom happens to have been
To slip a mackerel down a victim's pants.)
This year, I bow to fate and circumstance,
The hapless target of a crueler prank,
Though I don't even have myself to thank,
As Spring outside resumes its pointless dance.
Now is the season when the absent dead
Haunt us most vividly, amidst renewal:
Garlands of greenery adorn the head
Of every penitent, returning ghoul.
Rebirth awaits us in the days ahead?
Whoever said so was indeed a fool.

PALM SUNDAY

". . .the very stones would cry out. . ."
—Luke 19:40

I spend all day attempting to recharge—
Accomplish nothing—don't pretend to try—
Drawn blinds repel a vigorous blue sky
That proffers summer, even in late March.
Perhaps tomorrow morning I'll emerge,
Reluctantly discard this solitude;
It's nearly Easter, I should feel renewed;
Maybe I'll even make it back to church.
But Spring's an empty promise now, a tease,
A dusty, disappointed offering.
Buds burst like tumors on indifferent trees;
On windless days, the streets are barely breathing.
Proclaim your Resurrection, if you please—
No God of mine will rise from anything.

NO GRAVES WILL OPEN

"Heaven is at best here."
—Miller Williams

If there's a Heaven, where exactly *is* it?
And will our loved ones, lives distilled to light,
Find us so altered they recoil in fright?
What guarantees our golden robes will fit?
The old cosmologies refuse to quit:
That shining paradise, however bright,
Cannot withstand the onslaught of the blight;
Faith is, at best, a sort of tourniquet.
Beliefs, like paper lanterns, dim to gray,
Invisible against the white sunrise;
Dark brings a chilling promise of decay.
Yet rather this than such unlikely lies;
The dead blur into earth and fade away;
No graves will open, and no souls will rise.

YOUR UNFINISHED LIFE

Some damp spring morning, on an empty street,
Clouds opalescent with approaching dawn,
Young trees in leaf, the budding light replete
With possibility, you will be gone.
Consigned abruptly to oblivion,
You will not perish quietly in bed:
The clenched heart stills, and flesh turns carrion,
So much undone, the best words left unsaid.
Another moment might have served instead,
But *this* appointment no one can delay.
The rainy sky hangs heavy, dull as lead,
This final day, an ordinary day.
Let your unfinished life be epitaph:
You were not what you might have been—not half.

The Return of the Reverend Igneous Rock

"What doth the LORD require of thee, but to do justly, and to love mercy, and to walk humbly with thy God?"

—Micah 6:8

THE RETURN OF THE REVEREND IGNEOUS ROCK

He's vague about where,
precisely, he has been
for such an extended period of time.
Whispers among his congregants
insist he was whisked up to Heaven
to hobnob with the Lord Himself,
then returned to this world
as a living, breathing man—
a miraculous suspension
of accepted natural laws
that has only occurred
once before since the dawn
of recorded time. (And, to be
fair, there's a conflicting,
perhaps more plausible, rumor
involving an extended convalescence
following a difficult surgery
for an undisclosed complaint
at a hospital outside Memphis.)
His state of health is hard to fathom,
since the Reverend Igneous Rock,
his dark features the shifting
gray of pumice stone, can never,
strictly speaking, be said to be
"in the pink." At any rate,
it's clear he isn't telling—
and there's a righteous fire
in his eyes that discourages
too many questions.

BEULAH ROCK AND THE THREE-DOLLAR TURBAN

Only rarely will the pastor's wife—
a woman of unimpeachable dignity—
stoop to making a purchase
at the annual rummage sale,
but the instant she sees it
she knows she has to have it:

an antique flapper turban,
elastic still tight inside,
elaborately wrapped:
a shimmering helmet
of parrot-green cotton,
not the endless strip of silk
Sikhs must learn to tie.

Squinting into her compact,
Beulah admires the way
it enhances her features,
accenting the flecks
of dark gold in her eyes.

Arrayed in such incomparable finery,
she resembles Delilah or Salome—
perhaps a plump, particularly
imposing Queen of Sheba.

And *that*, of course,
is as it ought to be.
That is only fitting.

THE FORCE FAILS TO AWAKEN THE REVEREND IGNEOUS ROCK

This whole "Force" thing is,
in his opinion, a bit too Zen.
Cajoled into accompanying
Elijah and Myrtle to a matinée
at the local Cineplex, Igneous
finds himself most impressed
by the spacious reclining seats,
the daunting nearness of the screen.

The Reverend secretly misses Darth Vader,
who, despite his regrettable allegiance
to the Dark Side, possessed a stentorian voice:
an imposing figure whose stature
was worthy of a senior minister, and who,
moreover, always appeared attired in black.

(Perhaps a little pastoral counseling
would have sufficed to show the Sith Lord
the error of his ways, but *how* exactly,
Igneous can't help but wonder,
would one go about beating a light saber
into a ploughshare?)

And there's so much palaver
about the last Jedi he fears
that in this galaxy far, far away
the last Christian may—incredibly—
long since have gone extinct.

So Igneous sighs and reclines his chair,
settling into an anxious daydream
in which choirs of star-struck angels
serenade him from clouds
the rich golden color of buttered popcorn.

IGNEOUS ROCK AMONG THE LAGOMORPHS

For Cindy Sawchuck

A strong breeze animates enormous rabbits—
Canvas balloons—in front of City Hall,
Disturbing these strange traveling exhibits:
Their great ears tremble, but they do not fall.
Igneous Rock, bemused, cannot recall
A scene at once so comic and surreal;
He's not sure he's impressed by it at all,
Being half afraid of what it might reveal.
Does art *expose* truth, or does it *conceal?*
Lit like the ghost of Easters yet to come,
Such things may help the wounded world to heal—
And yet they leave the Reverend feeling lonesome.
He trudges back across the darkened lawn,
The first stars out, the sun already gone.

THE REVEREND IGNEOUS ROCK MAILS HIS INCOME TAX

He addresses two envelopes—
one to the Infernal Revenue Service,
the other to the French Eyes Tax Board—
then chuckles all the way to the mailbox.

THE REVEREND IGNEOUS ROCK WATCHES IT RAIN

The leaded glass in his window
only serves to further
blur an already indefinite sky,
a study in diluted grays,
and a backdrop
to the seemingly endless downpour.
It's been hissing down for weeks,
clearing only briefly,
and never for long.

Noah must have felt
something like this,
Igneous muses,
when the firmament roared
and rivers began
to overflow their banks
in those final hours before the deluge.
The heavens are meant to declare
the splendor of His handiwork,
but clearly Our Lord
is no watercolorist. The monotony
of the smudged light
that fills these afternoons
has become almost unendurable.

And at such times,
the dead draw near, unbidden.
They are in Glory,

the Reverend firmly believes,
but somehow they're here too—
as though this weather
has reluctantly granted them
a backward glance at the lives
they've left behind—
and however much he may aspire
to welcome and to comfort them,
even the Reverend Igneous Rock,
a man ever steadfast in his faith,
finds himself burdened
beneath the weight
of their unimpeachable sadness.

IGNEOUS ROCK AND EUSTACE TUBMAN

Eustace Tubman, noted ear nose and throat man,
pledges one of the more substantial tithes
swelling the coffers of Igneous Rock's
nondenominational neighborhood church.
The good doctor is very well thought of,
his diamond tie pin secretly the envy
of many a dapper Elder or Deacon.

But when the Reverend pays an office visit,
beneath the veneer of cordiality each is aware
of the other's wariness, a mutual skepticism,
and, on the physician's part, an unconcealed
note of scorn. The ringing in Igneous Rock's
ears is not the usual tinnitus, but the clamor
of great bronze bells—distant at first,
but growing more insistent as years pass.

IGNEOUS ROCK AND THE MERMAID

In a seldom-dusted corner
of Igneous Rock's study
is a lovely wooden statue
which might at first glance—
if anyone bothered to look at it—
seem more than a little out of place.
It's a mermaid, intricately
carved from monkeypod,
that Beulah bought for him
during their Hawaiian honeymoon
many more years ago now
than either cares to remember.
Mermaids must be, Igneous suspects,
a pagan symbol, none that he can recall
ever having been mentioned in Scripture.
No matter. It's an enduring reminder
of when he and Beulah were young.
And the sea nymph's broken fantail,
lovingly mended with carpenter's glue
after a rambunctious Elijah, aged two,
threw it to the floor during a tantrum,
gives the figure character, the Reverend
feels—a smidgen of personal history
enriching it beyond measure, beyond
anything the carver could have intended.

THAT PROFESSOR ON TV

That professor on TV—
you know, the one
in the wheelchair,
with the strange
electronic voice—
says that humanity
has a hundred years
at best, though he's
not sure whether
we'll be wiped out
by nuclear war,
global warming,
a genetically
engineered plague,
or a combination
of all three.

Igneous Rock hopes
with all his generous heart
that this is not the case.

Still, his voice trembles—
most uncharacteristically—
the following Sunday
as he reads aloud
from Malachi 4:1:

"For, behold, the day cometh,
that shall burn as an oven. . . ."

HOW KUMQUAT ACQUIRED HIS MONIKER

The Reverend Igneous Rock had a distant cousin
somewhere south of Memphis, an obscure Delta Bluesman
he met only once, as a child, and barely remembers.

Deaf Kumquat Washington was an anomaly in the genre,
a trombone player—by all accounts, an abysmally bad one—
who misleadingly styled himself as "King of the Slide."

Kumquat acquired his dubious moniker,
the story goes, because folks were convinced
no one possessed of a functioning pair of ears
could willingly have made such a dreadful ruckus.

It's rumored he tried to sell his soul
in a ghastly bargain at the crossroads
but the Devil wanted no part of the deal.
What became of him is anybody's guess.

Igneous recalls seeing one fragile acetate
the family would scarce have dreamt of playing
doing penance as a trivet or a serving tray
before being casually discarded with the trash.

All the Reverend knows for sure is this:
An ancient Getzen trombone, dented and dusty,
its dull gold worn to the bare brass in places,
lay neglected in the attic for decades,
until it was finally sold for a pittance
at the annual rummage sale.

BUNNY EARS

For Rev. John Buehrens

There's a tradition in his congregation:
They wear elaborate, even silly, hats
to celebrate the Resurrection Morning;
Igneous Rock has learned to live with that.
But how he ever wound up being persuaded
to preach a homily about the stone
faith rolled away, the daily miracle
that still sustains us in the risen Christ
while sporting these ridiculous pink ears
is more than even Igneous can fathom,
a frank assault to his great dignity.

The Reverend Rock has never really been
a man parishioners describe as stern,
and yet this floppy headpiece undercuts
the grandeur he must struggle to maintain
in ways his smart white suit cannot repair.

Although he knows that his Redeemer liveth,
and he stands tall and stalwart in the pulpit,
the tears that glisten on his broad black cheeks
can't truthfully be claimed as tears of joy.
Despite himself, in his mind's eye he sees
the inappropriate, stunned merriment
that twinkles in the eyes of the two women
as gleeful laughter fills the sepulcher—
their wonder momentarily forgotten,
even the fearsome Seraph chortling.

ELIJAH ROCK CONTEMPLATES FILLING HIS FATHER'S FOOTSTEPS

Elijah has just turned seventeen.
His father—who married late,
as his own father had before him—
is pushing seventy. Sometimes,
after the second service,
on yellow Sunday afternoons
when the sanctuary is empty
and he's certain the old man
isn't around to see or hear,
the boy climbs to the ornately
carved pulpit, feeling
varnish cool and smooth
beneath his fingers, light dripping
from ancient wood like fire
from molten glass. A fossilized
silence shudders as the Bible
falls open in his trembling
hands—with an apocalyptic boom—
but his voice, although already
a man's, is small and timorous,
faltering as he begins to read.

MYRTLE MAE ROCK SELDOM THINKS OF THE LORD

Being a pastor's daughter
can be burdensome
for a headstrong girl of fifteen—
especially when her father exudes
the kind of overwhelming aura
that always seems to surround
the Reverend Igneous Rock.

Myrtle Mae Rock
seldom thinks of the Lord,
being more preoccupied
with her smartphone,
"Desperate Housewives,"
and a growing collection
of shoes whose riotous
colors would have put
Noah's rainbow to shame.

Fortunately, Myrtle owns
an enormous "Hello Kitty"
backpack which she carries
everywhere and balances
on her broad lap in the pew
on Sundays, concealing
the fact that she spends
the entire service texting
her friends during her Dad's
interminable sermons.

A HAND-BLOWN BOTTLE

In a musty corner of the old parish hall
sits a bottle made of hand-blown cobalt glass,
empty for decades, its provenance forgotten—
it may have held one of the dubious remedies
some ancestor once peddled at minstrel shows.

Rarely, purely by chance,
light from the skylight
will happen to strike it:
For an instant it ignites
with a cool azure fire
that unfailingly causes
Reverend Igneous Rock
to pause for a moment
and marvel at this curio,
its glittering prophesies
fringed with blue silence.

IGNEOUS ROCK AND THE SNAKE HANDLERS

Some of the sisters in his congregation
swoon in the aisles and chatter in tongues,
as the Reverend Igneous Rock well knows.
But these strange rituals where serpents
flow in glistening metallic coils
over the bare arms of healers
make him uneasy, despite the fact
the practice is ostensibly Christian,
for in it he discerns traces of an older
tradition, a barbaric paganism redolent
of Canaanites, Hittites, or somebody.
The cold eyes of vipers, hard
as polished gemstones, quite frankly
give him the creeps; there's something
positively depraved in the way forked
tongues flicker with quick, salivary
fire, darting between wicked fangs.
And the snake handlers, deeply entranced,
are rarely bitten. Igneous shudders to think
of the eerie calm that somehow always
manages to keep a heinous death at bay.

IGNEOUS ROCK CONSIDERS POSTERITY

For Jeff Kalmar

Igneous Rock is not a humble man:
He advocates humility, but can
At times be more than slightly overbearing.

He knows his lofty place in God's Grand Plan,
Views mortal life as scraps left in the pan—
Though let it not be said that he's uncaring.

Today, the stained glass windows streaked with rain,
The Reverend grimly shoulders his Lord's pain;
And as the heavens groan beneath the weight
Of massive clouds as dark as churchyard slate,
He's sure the grateful accolades he's owed
Should rate (at least) one brief Pindaric Ode.

A CENTURY AGO

A century ago, Lucius Rock,
a skinny farm boy of sixteen
long before the unborn Igneous
was even a gleam in his future
father's eye, was wounded
by Klansmen, taking a bullet
in one shoulder that spread a stain
darker than Mississippi silt
across the tattered folds
of his shirt. He barely escaped,
hiding in a dry creek bed—
hardly daring to breathe
until the horses had passed,
the flicker of torchlight faded
into the dawn. To his dying day,
Old Lucius could feel the bite
of racist lead in his bones
whenever the moist white sky
hung low and swollen, ripe
with storms. The Reverend
Igneous Rock recalls the story,
abruptly, for no obvious reason,
on this dreary New Year's
when the clouds that gather
above the river are the color
of rust, their edges jagged,
heavy with hateful weather.

RECOVERING FROM A COLD, IGNEOUS ROCK UNWISELY LISTENS TO BLIND WILLIE JOHNSON

For Christopher Watkins

The Reverend still has more than a trace
of a sore throat and finds it impossible
to savor the raw, shredded vocals
of the late great Gospel Bluesman
without thinking how painful it would be
were he to attempt this style himself.

He's always been on the fence
regarding the old argument
that Blues is the Devil's music;
Blind Willie and Gary Davis
defy easy categorization
and would surely have to be,
if not admitted to the Kingdom,
at least allowed to loiter in the vestibule,
near enough to appreciate the choir.

Church music is undoubtedly superior
and certainly more suited to his own gifts,
but there are moments when he cannot
help but be drawn to the sonorous dusk
in which each plaintive blue note
shines as if by its own spectral light.

IGNEOUS ROCK IN THE WEE SMALL HOURS

Alone in the dark, long after Beulah
and kids have gone to bed, the Reverend
Igneous Rock—tie uncharacteristically
loosened—settles into the ancient recliner
in the den, its once fine leather cracked
and worn, taking out a carefully stashed
bottle and pouring himself a shot of Jack
and water, the Chairman's drink of choice.
Clearly a merciful Lord won't begrudge him
one slight indulgence after such an especially
diabolical day. The stereo's on, volume very
low, every pop and tick in decrepit vinyl
insistent, resonant in the surrounding stillness.
But as this damaged music washes over him,
decades dissolve and, gradually, he achieves
peace, sure of his prominence in the Grand Plan.
It's the Reverend's world. We just live in it.

DAVID BOWIE, NATALIE COLE, AND IGNEOUS ROCK

i.m.: Natalie Cole, died December 31, 2015
i.m.: David Bowie, died January 10, 2016

The Reverend's often heard rumored
celebrity deaths come in threes
and fervently hopes that, in this case,
the old superstition's untrue.
He and Beulah always enjoyed
Nat King Cole's flawless vocals
and welcomed Nat's daughter
into their record collection.
David Bowie's music is less familiar—
a bit too weird, and a little too *loud,*
for his staunchly conservative taste.
But Igneous knows any death
diminishes us all, and is especially
grieved whenever a musician is called
to join the ranks of the Celestial Choir.
He resolves to pray for them both,
partially consoled by the knowledge
that he himself still possesses a fair voice,
a rumbling bass that seems hewn
from the Rock of Ages, evoking
his unshakable family name.

IGNEOUS ROCK IS NO PHILOSOPHER

Preachers, as a rule,
are not existentialists,
focused as they must be
on awaiting the hereafter.
The Reverend Igneous Rock—
if he has ever bothered
to consider the matter at all—
probably thinks Sartre
is a popular seaside spa
favored by the well-to-do,
or else this evening's special
at a posh Parisian restaurant:
something he can't pronounce
and certainly wouldn't order.
But on a balmy February day,
even he is sometimes capable
of living in the here and now
and must admit, reluctantly,
that the pirouetting sunlight
on a new-thawed stream
inscribes upon the waters
its own bright Scripture—
a prophecy as stridently
joyous as the hosannas
of a thousand seraphim.

SUCH IS FAT(E)

(The Reverend Igneous Rock muses to himself.)

I'd hoped at least to cast a longer shadow
As youth deserted me and time wore on;
To my dismay, it simply isn't so;
I find, instead, I cast a *wider* one. . . .

THE PORTRAIT OF LORD JESUS

> *"There's a certain Slant of light,*
> *Winter Afternoons. . . ."*
> *—Emily Dickinson*

The ancient oil painting of Lord Jesus
facing the Reverend Igneous Rock's
imposing rosewood desk is old, possibly
older than the study's other furnishings;
at any rate, it is of similarly obscure origin.

Our Savior's slightly effeminate features,
darkened by several generations of dust—
for the portrait in its heavy gilded frame
has always been hung too high for even
the most fastidious housekeeper to reach—
present perhaps an even more inscrutable
expression than the artist originally intended.

But there is great kindness there,
and forbearance beyond the scope
of any ordinary mortal capacity;
Igneous has always been sure of that.

And sometimes—in late afternoon,
when the light turns golden and slants
through the heavy curtains at precisely
the proper angle—he seems to discern
an unmistakable smile of approbation,
a trace of pride, maybe even a hint
of quiet awe: enough to assure him
a lifetime spent doing good works
has not gone unnoticed on high.

CONCERNING ANGELS

Although she is usually loath to be seen
so scandalously under-dressed, Beulah Rock
actually owns—stashed in the back of a drawer
somewhere—a prodigious yellow tee shirt
bearing the slogan *I Believe in Angels*
in bold blue letters as vivid as a summer sky.
A gift from Myrtle several birthdays past,
it's aired out once a year, at the annual picnic.

Some insist that these celestial messengers are merely
symbolic, but she and the Reverend know better:
Many's the time, at dusk when the diminished light
transforms fields and trees to a brief, dusty gold,
she's sure she's heard them softly singing,
voices concealed behind the rustling leaves
or in the patient refrain of the nearby river.

A reassurance, perhaps a benediction,
the words are strange and vanish quickly,
like fragments of a conversation overheard
and then forgotten an instant before sleep.

IGNEOUS ROCK PERUSES THE FAMILY ALBUM

The oldest photos, daguerreotypes,
depict ancestors whose names
have long been lost, stern shades
in starched collars, whose eyes
shine like the night eyes of beasts,
as though they were caught
in a moment of stunned surprise
as the onrushing years ran them down.

In fading snapshots from the fifties,
a girlish Beulah and her late mother—
weighing nearly a thousand pounds between them—
beam for the camera, flowered sun dresses
struggling to restrain their unrepentant girth.

It's a family picnic, or some such.
Almost hidden in a corner of the frame
is a splinter of sunlight snared in the lens,
a ghostly rectangle of bleached brightness
Beulah used to tell the kids
was the Door into Heaven.

Polaroids taken in the sixties
have buckled and blistered
on the wide cardboard pages,
hinting those turbulent times
were singed by an unseen fire.

The final leaves are empty, forever unfilled.

Everything's digital nowadays, Igneous muses,
as if all our lives, at the instant they happen,
were already vapor, slipping through our hands.

IGNEOUS ROCK LAMENTS THE LAST ELECTION

As pastor of a strict Christian congregation,
Igneous Rock tends to be conservative—
but you have to draw the line somewhere.

The Reverend frets that the President-Elect,
aside from being so absurdly unqualified
to hold any public office, is basically an idiot,
spiritually bust as well as fiscally bankrupt,
a shameless bigot whose unexpected victory
was lauded by both the Nazis and the Klan.

In fevered dreams, he pictures legions barred
from "the land of the free," vainly struggling
to scale a concrete precipice rife with razor wire,
a behemoth that grows higher and more massive
until it turns away the sun, the very air itself.
(Perhaps the throng is desperate to escape.)

His own administration, Igneous feels sure,
would be more enlightened and compassionate,
a truer imitation of his Savior's gentle creed.

And his toupee would *certainly* be better.

IGNEOUS ROCK'S HIGH SCHOOL REUNION

The Gothic heap that was his alma mater
has grown a trifle musty through the years,
the hallways darker, vaulted ceilings lower
than he remembers on the rare occasions
he deigns to think about those days at all.
Surely the drinking fountains too are lower,
the oak doors narrower than once they were;
even the dingy amphitheater
where he slept through that dreadful science class
seems scarcely large enough to raise an echo.

Today he has returned, although nostalgia,
within the ordinary scheme of things,
is something he assiduously avoids.
He couldn't find the courage to refuse
when Mrs. Whip, his former principal—
translucent, shrunken, possibly more stooped,
but somehow not one bit less formidable—
requested that he offer up a prayer
such as befits a man of his high standing
before the graying compatriots of youth.

How long, exactly, has his exile been?
Out of respect for the good Reverend's pride
we must remain discretely imprecise
concerning just when he was graduated.
Suffice to say that he looks down his nose
at these young punks he passes in the hall
engrossed in disputations on Smart Phones,

more than a few of whom, in heedless haste,
have jostled him and nearly sent him flying—
gown, sash, gold-tasseled mortar board, and all—
to sprawl on newly-waxed linoleum.

Igneous Rock, staunch servant of the Lord,
would scarce have trembled in the lion's den
or faltered at the walls of Jericho.
How often, of a Sunday, he's addressed
much larger, and perhaps more hostile, crowds.
But this is not Judea, this is high school:
his footfalls prowl the endless corridors
past dented locker doors, the hoisted shields
of ranks of shadowy centurions.

In the gymnasium, the light is strong,
like torchlight in some heathen coliseum.
A sea of faces he no longer knows
look up expectantly, and he grows old.
Prim Leonetta Whip, her gaze severe,
seems set to mete out terrible punishments.
To his immense dismay he starts to sweat;
clutches, though it affords him no protection,
the suddenly diminished podium.
He sets aside his gilded calfskin Bible,
frozen before the waiting microphone—
a martyr pinioned on a cross of silence.

A PLAIN WOODEN CROSS

At ecumenical gatherings
hosted by other churches,
the Reverend Igneous Rock
has occasionally borne witness
to the agony of the pinioned Christ
depicted in intricately carved
crucifixes adorning the nave:
thorns on His brow black with blood,
dying eyes lifted heavenward,
transfixed by something
the mortal world cannot see.

The Reverend prefers
the modest simplicity
of the plain wooden cross
that graces the altar
in his own sanctuary:
how the crossbeam,
darkened by decades
of varnish, to the point
where the exact color
and nature of the wood
are impossible to guess,
seems—in its nakedness—
to invite each of us
to take our place there,
bearing a share of God's
unimaginable burden.

IGNEOUS ROCK AS A PAWN OF MEMORY

As we grow old, we gradually become
Wan, insubstantial phantasms like ghosts,
Though nothing supernatural marks this change—
A slow fuse in the marrow of our bones
Begins to incandesce, we feel diminished;
Increasingly we're pawns of memory.

Once proud of his prodigious memory,
Igneous Rock admits that he's become
Forgetful recently, his reach diminished.
He's even starting to believe in ghosts.
There's a reluctant creaking in his bones
That seems to herald a passage, a sea change.

He spends the plodding evenings like loose change,
Unable now to plumb his memory
For arcane texts, ephemera dry as bones.
Beulah and the two children have become
Mere interlopers, hesitant as ghosts,
Though Beulah's appetite hasn't diminished.

Midsummer's light, by autumn, has diminished,
Slipping toward shadows as the seasons change.
The vibrant lawns of childhood, green ghosts,
Glow in the far corners of his memory.
How pitiless the weather has become!
Great trees stand bare, denuded to their bones.

With every weird throw of the gambler's bones,

Inexorably, his flock has diminished,
For all his dreams of what they would become!
Collection plates that overflowed with change,
Packed Sunday services, are a memory.
Too many of his congregants are ghosts.

Igneous wonders, if not God, who ghosts
This script life keeps rewriting in his bones?
Should he commit his lines to memory?
After the Eucharist, he feels diminished.
Perhaps, in time, even our faith must change,
Accommodate the stranger we've become.

Perhaps we're blessed, if memory's diminished.
The Reverend, in his bones, accepts the change,
Discards his ghosts for what he must become.

The Fallow Heart: Villanelles

"The most beautiful people we have known are those who have known defeat, known suffering, known struggle, known loss, and have found their way out of those depths."

—Elisabeth Kübler-Ross

DAVE VAN RONK WAS FOND OF TULLAMORE DEW

For Christopher Watkins

To my delight, apparently it was true—
The Internet biographies inform me—
That Dave Van Ronk was fond of Tullamore Dew.

Dave was a Brooklyn bluesman through and through,
A folkie steeped in authenticity;
To my delight, apparently it was true.

I've long relied on booze and music, too;
And now I learn, somewhat belatedly,
That Dave Van Ronk was fond of Tullamore Dew.

He'd hoist the jug after a song or two,
Wetting his whistle not infrequently—
To my delight, apparently it was true.

All the performers of the era knew
His weathered voice owed something to the whiskey,
That Dave Van Ronk was fond of Tullamore Dew.

Since Dave embraced the same brand that I do,
I hasten to applaud his loyalty.
To my delight, apparently it was true
That Dave Van Ronk was fond of Tullamore Dew.

A WINTER SKY WITH ANSEL ADAMS CLOUDS

On days like this some caution is allowed:
The silver-gelatin terrain discloses
A winter sky with Ansel Adams clouds.

Deep silences declare themselves aloud,
Tucked in the petals of last summer's roses;
On days like this some caution is allowed.

This wind's particularly well-endowed,
And such aggressive weather presupposes
A winter sky with Ansel Adams clouds.

Embittered lessons can't be disavowed—
Perhaps the most inflexible of those is,
On days like this some caution is allowed.

One photograph would do the moment proud:
The Golden Gate, the Headlands, hold their poses;
A winter sky with Ansel Adams clouds.

Ashes enfold thin daylight like a shroud—
The aperture blinks once before it closes.
On days like this some caution is allowed,
A winter sky with Ansel Adams clouds.

THE MONKS OF SAN DURANTE

"Senza tema d'infamia ti rispondo."
—Inferno

The monks of San Durante-by-the-Sea
Relish the tarnished Adriatic light,
Sure of their garlands in Eternity.

Sorrow seeks solace in severity:
Stark cloisters and deep solitude delight
The monks of San Durante-by-the-Sea.

They wear their icy splendor easily,
Like constellations on a winter night,
Sure of their garlands in Eternity.

Their prayers are paeans to depravity;
The ravages of love will never blight
The monks of San Durante-by-the-Sea.

And in the final hour, says prophecy,
These damned will leave unholy graves to fight,
Sure of their garlands in Eternity.

Like their Dark Patron, they wait patiently
For the Great Cataclysm to ignite—
The monks of San Durante-by-the-Sea,
Sure of their garlands in Eternity.

THE FINAL DAYS OF THESE UNITED STATES

November, 2016

The final days of these United States,
These brief November evenings crisp with fear,
Seem to embrace the darkness that awaits.

There are no foreign hordes massed at the gates,
But danger threatens—it's already clear—
The final days of these United States.

The sudden frost no one anticipates,
The winter stars that sharpen and draw near,
Seem to embrace the darkness that awaits.

When any politician denigrates
The innocent, beneath their words I hear
The final days of these United States.

Yet casual friends and close associates—
Including some whom I hold near and dear—
Seem to embrace the darkness that awaits.

And after endless tooth-and-nail debates
The judgments grow increasingly severe.
The final days of these United States
Seem to embrace the darkness that awaits.

WHAT I RECALL MOST VIVIDLY IS SILENCE

Kennedy Assassination, November 22, 1963

What I recall most vividly is silence,
The sodden radiance beyond the windows:
What did I know, at six years old, of violence?

All down the unrelenting decades since
The horror of that moment only grows;
What I recall most vividly is silence.

Snared in the brutal jaws of circumstance,
A scared first grader faced confusing sorrow;
What did I know, at six years old, of violence?

Early dismissal offered me a chance
To flee the classroom, but nowhere to go—
What I recall most vividly is silence.

Never again would I experience
As raw a loss as that loss long ago;
What did I know, at six years old, of violence?

In recent days, there's ample evidence
We fare no better than the seeds we sow.
What I recall most vividly is silence;
What did I know, at six years old, of violence?

THE FALLOW HEART

These wings of sunlight powdering to dust
That beat against the numb late-summer sky
Know that decay does only what it must.

September now, when leaves begin to rust:
As autumn nears, it's pointless to deny
These wings of sunlight powdering to dust.

Time seems to nudge the blood with every gust—
But if the coastal breeze appears to sigh,
Know that decay does only what it must.

Eventually, we may learn to trust
The fallow heart—a kernel cracked and dry—
These wings of sunlight powdering to dust.

When our deceitful memories are thrust
Into a labyrinth love can't untie,
Know that decay does only what it must.

Earth is indifferent, her judgments, just;
As the corroded day descends to die,
These wings of sunlight powdering to dust
Know that decay does only what it must.

A GHOSTLY REMNANT OF A HOUSE NOW GONE

How strange to see this silhouette still there,
The shingled cottage recently torn down:
An ancient porch, an empty rocking chair.

Time managed damage nothing could repair;
Hard winter rains harsh reckonings have sown—
How strange to see this silhouette still there.

Like the detritus of some orphaned year,
Traces remain, forsaken and alone—
An ancient porch, an empty rocking chair.

The absent carpenters abandoned their
Apparently pointless labor at sundown;
How strange to see this silhouette still there.

Tonight the demolition site is clear;
Darkness and damp conspire to disown
An ancient porch, an empty rocking chair.

The image seems constructed to ensnare:
A ghostly remnant of a house now gone.
How strange to see this silhouette still there—
An ancient porch, an empty rocking chair.

HER HAPPY LIONS, ICED IN RED

i.m.: Genevieve "Mimi" Sparks, 1932–2016

Aunt Mimi's still alive inside my head
Although it's three days since she passed away;
I only learned tonight that she was dead.

No answer on the phone, my mother said.
A bad connection spelled a grim delay:
Aunt Mimi's still alive inside my head.

They found her—barely breathing—lying in bed,
Her lips and fingers blue. To my dismay
I only learned tonight that she was dead.

She'd turned aside from life, and dwelt instead
Inside her cluttered mind, her heart gone gray—
Aunt Mimi's still alive inside my head.

As, by a starry sky, we are misled,
Seeing the afterimage of decay,
I only learned tonight that she was dead.

I taste her Happy Lions, iced in red,
As though she'd baked them earlier today.
Aunt Mimi's still alive inside my head:
I only learned tonight that she was dead.

IN LESS THAN HALF A YEAR I WILL BE SIXTY

Colorado, December 22, 2016.

In less than half a year I will be sixty;
In subtle ways, at times I can't foretell,
I find that unexpected things transfix me.

December light looks on indifferently;
The winter has an acrid, barren smell;
In less than half a year I will be sixty.

A cottonwood, bent down arthritically,
Becomes a tortured soul in Dante's Hell;
I find that unexpected things transfix me.

Brown prairie winds disputing fitfully
Evoke the hollow tolling of a bell:
In less than half a year I will be sixty.

Is there still time to live authentically?
The brooding skies don't know—or they won't tell.
I find that unexpected things transfix me.

Forgive the seeming impropriety—
I can't buy what the Future has to sell.
In less than half a year I will be sixty;
I find that unexpected things transfix me.

A SILENCE FILLS THE CRATERS OF THE TONGUE

Once we accept that we're no longer young,
The heart contracts, not to expand again;
A silence fills the craters of the tongue.

Out in the open, where the light is strong,
The shadows sharpen, poised to hem us in,
Once we accept that we're no longer young.

In hidden rooms where none of us belong
The brutal rituals of grief begin—
A silence fills the craters of the tongue.

We join a rather melancholy throng,
Angels who lurch across a twisted pin,
Once we accept that we're no longer young.

The shriveled moon's an orphan in some song,
An olive in a glass of watered gin;
A silence fills the craters of the tongue.

Although there's nothing obviously wrong,
We feel a slow diminishment begin
Once we accept that we're no longer young:
A silence fills the craters of the tongue.

IT WILL GROW EVEN COLDER THAN WE KNOW

It will grow even colder than we know
When late December showers seethe offshore,
This coastal city where there is no snow.

When the defiant skies refuse to show
What dreariness the weather has in store,
It will grow even colder than we know.

Increasingly distrustful of tomorrow,
The rain-blurred lights on Union Square implore
This coastal city where there is no snow.

A vague malaise that only seems to grow,
A nagging fear we've never felt before—
It will grow even colder than we know.

Why celebrate a Savior long ago?
His mercy must have chosen to ignore
This coastal city where there is no snow.

Now every reassuring word rings hollow;
Our frail Republic's rotten to the core;
It will grow even colder than we know,
This coastal city where there is no snow.

THE SCULPTOR'S YARD

Today being the first day of February,
Winter assaults our always-sullen climate—
Wet weather sets a trap for the unwary.

In this thin drizzle voices do not carry;
The sodden atmosphere can't bear the weight,
Today being the first day of February.

Whatever outworn hopes the month may bury
Beneath a sky as gray and worn as slate,
Wet weather sets a trap for the unwary.

The moss-blind eyes of shattered statuary
Look to the hard snows of an eastern state,
Today being the first day of February.

But our supposed "seasons" never vary;
Regardless of the forecast—or the date—
Wet weather sets a trap for the unwary.

The sculptor's yard beside the mortuary
Is vacant now, abandoned to its fate.
Today being the first day of February,
Wet weather sets a trap for the unwary.

YOUR DEATH STILL FEELS IMMEDIATE TODAY

i.m.: Patricia Lewis Smith, 1953–2005

Eleven years ago you passed away,
Succumbing to the rupture in your brain;
Your death still feels immediate today.

Rumors of light begin to pierce the gray,
But one blunt fact seems fated to remain:
Eleven years ago you passed away.

I've never been the sort of man to pray
To absent deities, although it's plain
Your death still feels immediate today.

A resolutely ordinary day,
The evening—like this evening—stained with rain:
Eleven years ago you passed away.

Low breathing stirred the silence where you lay
Beyond the reach of anything but pain.
Your death still feels immediate today.

Christmas just past, the nascent hour held sway,
And yet it seemed the future had been slain.
Eleven years ago you passed away:
Your death still feels immediate today.

SOMETIMES THE SKY IS PLIANT

"I will not make a sonnet from
Each little private martyrdom."
—Joseph Auslander

Sometimes the sky is pliant, sometimes stone,
Porcelain blue, or grim, obdurate gray.
We're passing strangers, bound for parts unknown.

Each of us is essentially alone,
Despite what old religions always say.
Sometimes the sky is pliant, sometimes stone.

And what is Truth except an old soup bone
After the marrow has been boiled away?
We're passing strangers, bound for parts unknown.

Hope's an illusion, clumsily outgrown;
The day we die, an ordinary day.
Sometimes the sky is pliant, sometimes stone.

No monument, and no way to atone
For any harm we caused, to our dismay
We're passing strangers, bound for parts unknown.

Though from the rocks themselves our shrouds be sewn,
All things in time fall victim to decay.
Sometimes the sky is pliant, sometimes stone;
We're passing strangers, bound for parts unknown.

THE CLOAKED EROTICISM OF ROSE WINDOWS

". . .the soul illuminated its hair for a second. . . ."
—Allen Ginsberg, HOWL. Part I

Miracles falter where the light is strong;
Gold flakes and frays from sagging wooden haloes.
Love and religion—neither holds us long.

Halfhearted rags of petulant plainsong
Affix themselves to something in the shadows—
Miracles falter where the light is strong.

There comes a moment when belief seems wrong;
Eventually, boredom will expose
Love and religion—neither holds us long.

The architects of faith knew all along
What every shady sidewalk prophet knows:
Miracles falter where the light is strong.

Hidebound traditions struggle to prolong
The cloaked eroticism of rose windows:
Love and religion—neither holds us long.

The soul unbinds its tresses for the throng,
Each shining strand a filament that glows.
Miracles falter where the light is strong;
Love and religion—neither holds us long.

Curios: Previously Unpublished Poems, 1976–1987

"Ask me who I was."

—Marley's ghost

THE WEDDING

i.m.: Adrienne Stengel, 1958–2006

There's your bright breath,
A bride's veil, dispersing.

The tear-drop heart,
Luna's dark oyster.

The moon, a ring
Of pale blue stone

Cracking,
Borrowing light;

The plate where
The wedding guest

Watches his face
Grow old.

There are dry leaves and wires
Vaulting an aisle;

The asphalt,
Black velvet.

A bat's twittered blessing
Under a streetlight.

Lastly, the trees
Holding their peace,

The hushed futility
Of vows.

LULLABY AND DIRGE

Once a day it happens,
always on time:

The night comes down,
swift as a stone.

Under its weight,
your first shoes turn to bronze;

the bride's straw flowers
ignite, becoming stars;

your ancestors' bones
rock uneasily on their porches,

blank grins
full of gold.

Sometimes the darkness
moves in a wall across the fields,

like a storm front,
a tidal wave:

those it surprises
can only stand and wait—

open-mouthed,
frozen with hoe and shears:

a crow nodding
on either shoulder.

SCÈNE DE GENRE

A stark, white room,
bare except for a table.

A rough wooden table,
cracked and stained.

The round peasant's-bread
like a moon in its center.

A woman cutting a cross
into the loaf, for the dead.

The rood which blackens
under her furrowed skin

like the shadow of
some monstrous bird.

APPLE TREES

Cold Soil Road, Lawrenceville, New Jersey, 1984

Since this is February
their branches now
thin to a nothingness
through which wind whistles.

They nod like old women
in the cold sunlight,
casting hideous shadows
across the ditches.

How easy to imagine
they once were witches
surprised by the sun
at some pagan rite.

And now I seem to see
some zealous preacher
of the nineteenth century
striding among them.

Vainly he gesticulates,
the pages of the Bible
he cradles in his palm
flapping in the wind.

NEW WORLD

"Concerning Lions, I will not say that I ever saw any myself."
—William Wood, New England's Prospect, *1639*

It wasn't the Eden we'd thought.

We arrived in the dead of winter:
Ponds and streams were clogged with ice.

That spring, the soil brought forth
stones, and sharp hooks of yellow bone.

Some said these were Satan's teeth,
and prayed fervently. Lions were heard

in the black underbrush within a mile
of Plimouth. Their howling surprised us

at prayer: The pale wings of open Bibles
beat in our hands. Hymns rose like smoke.

ANSWERING THE RIDDLE

The egg arrives first,
by bus.
Response to an anonymous
phone call.

The chicken is late,
has come on foot,
crossed many roads
to get here.

A grimy corner
by a Seven-Eleven,
darkness falling,
large raindrops.

Neither knows
why they have come,
what this will accomplish.

The chicken ruffles her feathers,
struts impatiently,
stamps out a smoldering butt.

The egg of course is silent,
translucent,
moon-like in the gloom.

Inside the shell,
a phone is ringing.

PRIMER

First page almost blank
for the years
you can't remember.
A spot in one corner:
ink, dust, a fly?

Next, names of flowers:
silver bell
trout lily
bachelor's button.
This page is meadow green.
A breeze lisps your name.

Women's names now.
Audrey, dark eyes.
Rain in Erica's hair.
Rachel gathers wild mint.
Ruth feeds sparrows.

The lists get harder.
Words like
derelict, exile.
Words it may take
lifetimes to learn.

Lastly, the words
an old man says in his sleep
on long nights
when winter thickens

at his window
and there is none to hear.

THE PEACEMAKERS

New York, June 12, 1982

Above the bristling crowd,
choppers dart like startled bees
between towers with a sun
in every window.

If the world must end,
let it end now—
with bagpipes, singing,
ribbons, bright balloons.

If the wind
blows flesh away,
our bones will lie down
on Second Avenue,
hand in hand.

When darkness fills
the emptied city,
they will keep shining.

AUDLEY END

i.m.: Franz Wright, 1953–2015

In a fountain
you see your face:
skull white,
a tourist's penny
in each eye.

Who comes a visitor
to a palace
without dressing
for the dead?

They smile
from every wall.

Look how they welcome you
into silk chairs,
canopy beds
fringed with dust.

Here you can dream
the dead's dreams
which are like those
of the blind from birth.

HEARSES

Let us begin
with the tassels
for the undertaker's horse,
hung on a rack
in a dim garage.

The high wooden hearses
are here too,
shining like leather
in the gloom.

They're the kind
that still have
those brass candle holders.

The velvet curtains
are pulled aside
enough to allow
just a glimpse
into each dark interior,
into things to come.

Of course they're empty.
There's nobody here but me,
and I wandered in
by mistake.

NOCTURNE

Hoboken, New Jersey, 1983

I wake before dawn,
suddenly sure
that another
is also awake,
wandering now
down ruined avenues,
past houses
dark with sleep.

The moon leans
over his shoulder,
a dusty mirror
just out of reach.

Why do I feel
his presence
so strongly,
his immense loneliness?

When I go to the window
the street is empty.

It's bitterly cold.
Light slants
through blinds
into the room,
leaving long scars
on the walls.

WATCHING A BLIND MAN IN A SUBWAY STATION

What appalls
is how the white cane
hovers a moment
in the vacant dark
above the tracks
still trembling with departure.

In dreams I sometimes become
the one I have so often seen,
my eyes the empty moons
hidden behind his black glasses.

Mine too are the first
hesitant steps
on the metal stairs,
among the throng whose faces
are turning to stone.

KNIFE GRINDER

Consider that figure
from childhood,
the old man arriving
just at dusk
in an ancient jeep,
ringing a bell.

How solemn we must have seemed
as we gathered
the kitchen knives,
blades flashing
in the sunset.

We watched like worshipers
as he bent over the wheel,
blue sparks flying
into the dark.

He sang as he worked,
in a language no one knew.
His song seemed to be
the knife of longing
sharpened for us all.

THE UNFINISHED THRONE

Convinced that the Judgment was imminent, James Hampton began in 1950 to construct an elaborate throne room for Jesus in a rented garage in Washington, DC.

He dreams of bright rolls of tinfoil,
the garage with its dirty light, the low,

bare ceiling beams. Endless patterns
in smeared chalk, shears clipping thin,

wrinkled metal into triangles, diamonds,
dove's wings. Hours of patient folding,

his quick fingers bent in a constant,
dancing prayer. The work whose details

he mouths like a litany. Daily, the dark
odor of glue intoxicates him: an incense.

Then he begins to die. There at the foot
of the unfinished throne, among glittering

piles of scepters and cardboard crowns.
His body used up, stunned by familiar glory.

And the folded cot in one corner spreads
to receive him like a pale, upturned palm.

THE FLOWER BURNING

In all the coastal villages
they are burning flowers.
Soldiers ease dark trucks
through narrow, twisting streets,
past shuttered houses with low tile roofs.
Flanked by motorcades,
convoys hurry along a mountain highway.
Below, the cliffs plunge
into a faded sea.

A barbed-wire fence
surrounds the abandoned scrapyard.
In the towers, guards
clutch machine guns.
It is here that the flower burning
will take place.

The scrap heaps are covered with bright petals,
still damp in the first
gray light. You hear the gruff
idling of engines
as headlights are switched off.
The heavy sweetness
of thousands of flowers
hangs over everything.

The ovens have been glowing
all night long.
Rows of men in greasy overalls

shovel roses and sweet rocket
into the flames.

When morning comes, bony children
throng around the fence,
ragged and barefoot.
Their wide eyes shine
and flicker.

Above them, great columns of smoke
knot into dark blossoms.

DANCE OF THE DRESSES

For Elizabeth Hornor Boquet

Nights are lonelier
since your father left.
Now, the divorce final,
you sometimes tiptoe
to your mother's room,
knowing she is lonely too.
She sleeps on her side:
Your girlish body
fits snug against hers,
your feet reach past her knees.
Waking a little, she
rubs a hand through your hair.
Tonight the closet door
quietly slides open:
her dresses, empty,
waltz through the room,
hollow skirts and blouses
filled exactly to her shape.
Mom, you whisper,
the dresses are dancing.
Nuh, she says, barely stirs.
But she sees them too.
Rehearsing old steps
from memory, open sleeves
embracing an absence.

IF I HAD MY DRUTHERS

The dead would
bury us.

They'd erect
in our memory
the stony life's-head,
its eyes swollen
like ripe apples.

Our bodies
would be leaves
drifting
on a dark river,
all their color
washed away.

The carousing dead
would dance above us
in the heavy,
tramping wind.

Fickle Weather: Recent Free Verse

"There are some things you learn best in calm, and some in storm."

—*Willa Cather*

A POSSIBLE STARTING POINT

Flame trees flaring against a heatstroke sky
ignite on the borders of my earliest memories
but are not consumed. Guam: I'm barely four.
After more than half a century what I recall
most vividly is a water buffalo—in Chamorro,
a *carabao*—bathing beneath a rural bridge,
its broad back dripping, fierce with light.

TASTES LIKE CHICKEN

Even on a hog farm in Nebraska
in the depths of the Depression
Rachael was a normal thirteen-year-old
who sometimes ignored her chores,
forgot to take care of what little she had.
And when she neglected Sally,
the Holland Lop she raised from a kit,
whose dark, ticked fur made her look
from a distance more cat than rabbit,
the family, always pressed for food,
quietly slaughtered the animal,
saying nothing to the unsuspecting child.
"Have some chicken," they coaxed,
passing the basket around at supper,
a checkered cloth concealing breaded flesh
that could have been most anything.
Uncle Silas laughed and laughed
as Rachael took her first bite.

A PUZZLE BOX

i.m.: Leonard Cohen, 1934–2016

I will make for your death
a small, sturdy poem,
like a puzzle box—
sandalwood maybe,
sanded smooth, but unvarnished,
sufficient in its nakedness.
It will retain about it
a smell of spices,
cloves and chicory,
long since crumbled
into dust. You once wrote
that some men deserve
mountains, and you do,
but I cannot offer you one.
I'll design instead for the occasion
a poem constructed like
a simple, inscrutable object—
a thing whose completeness
you would have appreciated.

DECORATION DAY

The film *Gone With the Wind*
being as distant from us now
as the Civil War itself was
at the time of the movie's
original theatrical release,
I spend all afternoon
watching yet another
newly restored version,
musing that my mother
insisted she remembered
elderly men in mended uniforms—
blue and gray gathered side by side,
their ranks quietly diminishing—
laying wreaths on already
crumbling gravestones
on Decoration Day
in Depression-era Ohio.

CHECKING

Startled awake, I see him
hunched over his walker
in the darkness, shrunken,
ghost-pallid even in shadow.
He has mistaken the room
I'm using for the bathroom,
as he does nearly every night.
"Are you okay, Dad?" I ask,
loud enough for him to hear.
"Just checking on you,"
he says, the lie obvious
to us both. He has no idea,
at all anymore, where he is.

WE CAN'T BE SURE

Dad, there are times when your eyes
shine with a momentary clarity
that almost makes it possible to believe
you are the man we remember,
that you remember us.
The beard an aide
at the assisted living facility
shaved off because of a misunderstanding
has mostly grown back now,
if paler than it was,
adorning a face
ever more translucent and ghost-like.
We can't be sure how much of you is there,
or for how much longer—
we take each day's uncertainty as a gift,
knowing the days ahead, at best, are few.

DEATH WATCH

The hospice nurse thinks Dad
may have had a stroke, since
his pupils aren't the same size,
although Mom suspects this
could be only a residual result
of cataract surgery several
years ago. Abruptly, his blood
sugar, checked on a whim,
tops 700, but an insulin shot
does nothing to bring him
to himself. Once again the family
begins a death watch, for the sixth
time in less than a year. He's grown
unresponsive, if not actually technically
comatose. Then, the following
morning, he's alert and talking,
and the whole process repeats itself.

CLING, IF YOU MUST

Cling, if you must, to the future
long imagined, the life where
you would always have a place.
But know the day will come
when you will be startled
by a stranger in your mirror,
features pallid and drawn,
rapidly dissolving in the cold.
You recognize him already
in what your father has become—
a shriveled interloper in darkness,
the rooms of the tiny apartment
suddenly unfamiliar, simple things
grown difficult—walking, urinating,
the very act of expelling the faint,
hesitant plume of his breath.

RISING TOWARD RADIANCE

i.m.: Dr. C. Lavett Smith, 1927–2015

Dad, the news of your passing this evening
is the first indication we've had in months
that your condition has finally stabilized.
It's hard to grieve when much of who you were
has already been gone for so long:
the brilliant intellect dwindling
like a glimmer of sun on a dark pond,
or the wake of a skiff you might have piloted
through tropical waters you once explored.
You were never a religious man;
your body will probably be cremated;
no sort of service has been planned.
But in the few photographs that remain—
all that we really have of you now—
you look like a diver even on dry land:
muscled and dark-haired in early pictures,
suggesting the past is deeply submerged;
emaciated and pale in more recent shots,
your fragile limbs swollen with light
as though in these final months you'd been
swimming away from the finality of death,
rising toward a radiance beyond any language.

ENTERING THE TOMB

Three days after his eighty-seventh birthday
my father receives a call from a friend
in New York as I'm sitting next to him
and my mother at the senior housing facility
in Fort Collins where they have moved
to be nearer to my sister's family.
We can hear only his side of the conversation.
He remembers his former student, and seems
glad to hear from him, but says abruptly,
"We're not in Fort Collins anymore; actually,
I have no idea where the hell we are."
(He has hardly ever sworn in his long life.)
He hands the cell phone back to Mom
with the bewildered air of an archaeologist
who, upon entering the tomb, is confronted
by an artifact both ancient and inscrutable,
whose function, forgotten for millennia,
he can't begin to fathom or to guess.

THE FLAMES THAT CLAIMED HIM

Increasingly, these past few years,
I have seen my father's face
in the bathroom mirror:
in my thinning hair, my beard
dimmed to the color of dust.
My gaze, blue as cold weather,
has begun to shine with
something I can't quite name,
a yearning I seem to recognize.
But now that he's gone,
the worn out limbs
glowing at last like the matchsticks
they had come to resemble,
the brain, a spent vessel finally unable
to hold his cluttered memories,
reduced by the gas jets
to a smoldering puddle
and eventually evaporated,
I see in my matinal reflection
traces of the flames that claimed him,
the glint in my eyes no longer
hope but the beginnings
of a conflagration, as though
the spark of his death had lit a fuse
somewhere deep within me.
Someday perhaps I will be
cremated as well, my ashes
mingled with those of my late wife,
scattered on the winds above the Golden Gate.

MY FATHER'S ASHES

My father's ashes came from the mortuary
in a black velvet box my mother
promptly hid from view in a closet.
They're all that she has of him now,
after his ordeal by fire and grinding:
a thin gray dust as delicate as smoke.
The housekeeper responsible for her hallway
at the retirement home made a point
of mentioning she wouldn't be disturbed
by the knowledge they were there.
Many apartments she cleans, she informed
Mom, accommodate the cremated
remains of the residents' loved ones.
It wouldn't be a problem, she insisted,
absolutely no problem at all.

L. FRANK BAUM'S FINAL WORDS

L. Frank Baum, architect of Oz,
died in 1919 in a modest bungalow
in Hollywood, in a room papered
with images of chrysanthemums
like those he had tended and loved.
His eyes, at the last, were clear
and unafraid. "Now," he said softly,
"we can cross the Shifting Sands."

THE WEATHER HERE DOESN'T COUNT FOR MUCH

My great grandmother, Mrs. B. Y. Harrison, burned much of the family memorabilia in the early 1950s.

The weather here doesn't count for much.
A halfhearted drizzle falls through soiled light
the color of a photograph left in a bonfire,
although the face in the snapshot is a stranger:

a severe young woman with tentative eyes,
in a dress already unfashionable decades ago,
the flowered wallpaper behind her darkened,
curling, singed a little around the edges.

Were there really a fire, I'd guess incessant rain
must long since have extinguished the flames,
but this blaze keeps smoldering only in memory—
and the weather here doesn't count for much.

THROUGH THE WINDOW

Raindrops on cold glass
trace the memory of light
momentarily.

AN OLD SAW

An old saw insists every time you shiver
someone is stepping on the precise spot
one day destined to be your grave.

Sooner or later a moment arrives
when whatever you are
is all you are ever going to be.

And you *do* shiver,
as though a cloud
had hidden the sun.

But the sky is clear:
warm air lightly scented,
trees ripe with nascent light.

A BRIEF GEOLOGY OF DEATH

For Robert Crabill

Marble and granite, slain for tombs,
carve easily, the minerals firmed
by unseen pressures in the earth.
Slate, softer, yields gently
before the sculptor's chisel,
but will serve for monument
when used to mark a gentle,
unassuming life. All, however,
wait on the whim of the weather,
every inscription composed
of serifs and down strokes
rain rounds at first, softens,
and blurs eventually into silence.
When it comes to remembrance
these man-sown stones won't do.
Turn instead to the boulders,
the hidden ruptures in the landscape,
the folds and concealed seams
that lie deepest, wrought
by the hand of time itself.
Only the most patient among us
will learn to read what's written
there, epitaphs older than language
and surely destined to outlast it.

GRAFFITI

Spray painted on a bus stop trash
can, in jagged strokes that powder
at the edges, we find these words
glowing like a passionate arpeggio
against the dullness of the dented
metal: *Miles Davis Lives!* It's high
noon in the city, and for a moment
the sky, golden with snared heat,
shines like the bell of a trumpet.

THE LAST BLACKSMITH

This late in August the light turns golden
South of Market, falling on warehouses,
boutiques, and chic Peruvian restaurants.
From a Transbay bus—incredibly—
we glimpse a blacksmith's shop,
the unassuming wooden building
squaring its shoulders by the freeway,
painted anvil gray as though poised
to beat the fire from a molten sky.

WALKER

"Walk-*ER!*," exclaims the lad
whom Scrooge dispatches
to purchase the prize turkey
hanging in the Poulterer's
in the next street but one.
The unfamiliar term is,
confides the glossary
of my Penguin paperback,
"A Victorian cockney expression
indicating bemused incredulity."
Recovering from a back injury,
I address it now—grudgingly—
to this wheeled contraption
I have become so reliant upon
for my every hesitant step.
Me using a walker? "Walk-*ER!*"

EMPTY STADIUM AT NIGHT

For Laurie Sato

There's a holiness here,
a pious quality of silence,
sacramental reassurance
in the smell of recent rain.
On a moonless December night,
the huge screen of the Jumbotron
is doubled in water submerging the line
between third and home—
a plane of twitching color,
vibrant with season's greetings,
that strangely appears plain white
in every cell phone photo we take.
And in the upper tiers, banks of seats
slant skyward toward the darkness
like a congregation full of penitents
absolved by the outfield lights.

A FRAGMENT OF THE BUDDHA'S SKULL

Archaeologists found the remains of Buddhist saints, including a parietal bone that inscriptions say belonged to the Buddha himself.
—*Fox News*

This holiest of relics is after all
only a brittle shard of dry bone,
a monastery of empty cells
abandoned on the molecular level,
curved like a fragment of eggshell
or a brown evening sky,
Enlightenment lying in the realization
that it is just another manifestation
of the humble, ubiquitous dust.

AIRBORNE

For Carrie Knowles

According to one ancient Chinese legend,
the clouds are solid, covered in coarse grass,
with hidden caves, benevolent dragons
well-versed in eerie, esoteric arts.

Airborne among heaped, luminescent whites
that bleed to gray in places at the edges,
how easily we might suppose such splendor
comprised a sort of vaporous frontier
beyond whose shining borders none dare cross.

AFTER THE FLOOD

"If you go down in the flood
It's gonna be your fault."
—Bob Dylan

I'll celebrate the songster's seventy-fifth
with MP3s on infinite repeat,
revisiting for the first time in decades
derided works alongside the iconic.

The cover photo from *Before the Flood,*
raised lighters like a starry summer sky—
luminous on the dimming monitor—
offered no shelter from the rising storm.

The urgency that animates the Band
on that live set from forty-odd years ago
foretells a deluge doomed to sweep away
more than we ever could have realized.

These shades we feel we ought to recognize
are only younger versions of ourselves
who let the years engulf them, unaware
they were already drenched in a hard rain.

THE SURREALIST IN LOVE

"A woman waits for me. . . ."
—Walt Whitman

It begins with a vast calamity of wings,
a night sky blooming like a black dahlia.
She descends from somewhere above,
a feather or leaf inscribing pirouettes
on wind from a slaughtered country
whose stale breath disgorges the tiny,
threadlike bones of extinct tropical fish.
Swollen, the twin moons of her breasts
orbit each other, bathed in their own light.
Already her toes are putting down roots,
groping their way through the darkness
beneath every shuddering pavement.
And she has begun, rapidly, to grow.
When her body is spacious enough,
she will eventually *become* the world,
the curve of her thighs glowing blue
like the horizon observed from space.

FICKLE WEATHER

From a plane above the Colorado plains

Altitude does little to diminish
Grimness in the fallow fields below—
Nothing is concealed by sooty snow,
Only some momentary feints at purity.
Still, I'd like to think some watershed,
Tentative, but undeniable, awaits;
I find myself oddly hopeful, despite
Conventional distrust of fickle weather.

HENRY, WALT, AND BRAM

Bram Stoker, whose suppressed homosexuality
is implicit in the horror with which women
are regarded in *Dracula,* wrote long, gushing
letters to Walt Whitman as a young man, praising
the poet's understanding of "men like ourselves."

The older writer responded with bewildered
kindness, flattered perhaps by the adulation,
but rightly suspicious of its callow sincerity.
The two never actually met; shortly thereafter,
Stoker fell under the spell of the flamboyant

Shakespearian actor Sir Henry Irving, who
sported a deep black velvet cape, and strode
through gaslight with preternatural assurance,
while the stage manager fluttered around him
like a moth drawn to an incinerating flame.

The rest is buried between the lines, interred
in the "decrepit earth" of the nineteenth century.
No consummation ever occurred that we know.
Twelve novels and three short story collections
were disregarded, unmentioned in any obituary.

THE RESONANCE OF ANGUISH

I'm deeply moved by *Set Fire to the Stars:*
The Welshman playing the lead embodies Thomas—
Exudes a whiskey-soaked exuberance—
And the stark settings, naked black and white,
Transport us instantly to 1950.

But when the film concludes I turn once more
To those old Caedmon records I still love,
Dismissed by some as pompous and bombastic,
But bearing nonetheless, it seems to me,
Their own improbable magnificence.

The resonance of anguish in that voice
(As captured by an ancient microphone)
Reverberates across the shackled years—
Making of the hurt heart a crucible,
Recasting the ineffable as art.

CONCEALED

i.m.: Patricia Lewis Smith, 1953–2005

The moon a brass nail
hammered into the night.
The landscape beneath,
draped in crisp snow,
like a house abandoned,
drop-cloths on all the furniture.
Or like your face concealed
under a mortuary sheet—
a deepening darkness
colder and more still
than this windless prairie
tonight, on the ninth
anniversary of your death.

FOUR CLERIHEWS

For Chris Charles

1\.
William Hartnell's Doctor Who
Was a codger through and through,
But his jaunts through space and time
Nearly always were sublime.

2\.
Bela Lugosi—
Why do you suppose he
Never hit it off
With Boris Karloff?

October 31, 2016

3\.
Macabre Edgar Allan Poe
Was quite the drunkard, as we know,
By turns aggressive, maudlin, and pathetic—
Or maybe he was simply diabetic.

4\.
I'm most gratified, it's true,
To learn about the clerihew—
Very soon I may be able
To use the word when playing Scrabble.

THE POET AS FISHERMAN

Honoring Stuart Friebert.

Eighty-five now, he smiles almost benignly
from the back of his most recent collection:
white hair thinned at last to recollected light,
features translucent but still recognizable,
slightly flattened nose I always suspected
must once long ago have been broken.

Sagacity struggles with a trace of smugness
in his expression, betraying firm certainties
concerning the state of contemporary poetics.
It's all there, he seems to be saying, a favorite
expression in freshman workshops at Oberlin,
those days, incredibly, nearly forty years ago.

And so it is. I find in these late poems clarity
sometimes lacking in the books of the nineties:
Once again he confidently reels the reader in
like an expert fly fisherman casting his lines,
well-honed words full of buoyancy and glitter,
images bobbing like brightly colored lures
through the murk of our often negligent tongue.

SEVENTEEN BELOW

On I-25 near Denver,
wind smokes the ice
from the asphalt,
a dozen tiny squalls
scattered by our tires.

It's seventeen below,
though in this dry climate
the temperature is insidious
and one can freeze to death
without ever feeling cold.

On the horizon,
the sky is low, metallic,
filled with squalid light
where a few brown flakes
drift like ashes.

These are the final days
of a mean year;
death stalks my ailing father,
but—so far—keeps its distance,
confident of eventual victory.

In the driver's seat, you
quietly endure chronic pain,
eyes fixed on the road
along which cottonwoods
bend to a blustery martyrdom.

Neither of us is sure
of anything now;
we have only this weather,
this bitter radiance
through which we travel.

LYING IN BED

I've been thinking about
this respiratory infection
like a damp avalanche
in my lungs for weeks,
considering the mundane
misery of an afternoon
which announces itself,
through drawn blinds,
as achingly clear light,
in spite of everything.

EARLY NOVEMBER LIGHT

i.m.: Patricia Lewis Smith, married 11/7/98, died 12/27/05

On afternoons like this, early November light
acquires a heft that would have startled
Emily Dickinson, that pale shade in crinoline
who understood the weight of silences.

Wind stirs in leaves barely fringed with yellow,
a timid fire more verdigris than gold
that smells of a misremembered season,
and something ancient awakens in you.

It resembles the moment you first realize
that love, like its darker twin, loss, is a hook
sunk deep in the heart, shrapnel
from a blast you never saw coming.

DEAD PHONE BOOTH

Ragged, down at the heels,
he's always nattily attired
in a suit coat, year round,
whatever the weather—
even if the twill *is* dusty,
a trifle frayed at the cuffs.

He carries a dead cell phone
into which he speaks urgently
as he wanders past queues
of derelict warehouses,
negotiating weighty deals
with persons unknown.

It's whispered in the neighborhood
by those who've seen for themselves
that in the days before cell phones
he used to conduct his business
from an abandoned phone booth,
the phone ripped out ages ago.

DAYBREAK IN ALABAMA

In reply to Langston Hughes

I have never been to Alabama
but, over the course of sixty years,
borne witness to daybreak
twenty-one thousand nine hundred times.
I remember how, in the East Coast
cities of my youth, tenement
windows burst into molten gold,
the moment pinioned in time, quivering
like the stillness in the grandest music.
I see no reason why daybreak in Alabama
should be any less memorable, any less
compelling, than daybreak elsewhere.
Yet I also know there are days
when night gains the upper hand
even in skies so cloudless and clear
you can taste the ripe light on your tongue.

A MAN SELLING WHIPS ON CHRISTMAS EVE

New York, 1983

I'd say by now he must be half-frozen,
there on the rapidly darkening sidewalk
where the shop windows are dimming
as the grilles are lowered for the night,
and it's just starting, hesitantly, to snow.

His arms must ache from swinging
the slick tendrils of braided leather;
his voice has certainly grown hoarse
from calling out to dubious passers-by
that whips make wonderful Christmas gifts.

Maybe he's even begun to believe it
as black tongues crack against the concrete,
shoppers scurry past: Maybe at this hour
every one of them resembles his abusive father
or a woman he loved who married someone else.

And with each thrust he pictures flayed coats,
shredded parkas hemorrhaging eiderdown,
the cold air swirling with feathery carnage
while on the next corner, cheerfully oblivious,
a Salvation Army band mangles "Jingle Bells."

ETERNITY DEEPENS TO TEAL

In the Sunset, a district
ironically given to mist
and almost bereft of sun,
summer is the coldest season.
One can smell the weariness
of the sea even on streets
where the shore is too distant
to be visible. Surf and sky
are the uniform monochrome
of fading photographs
or of the first flickering,
tentative years of television.

I did not come here
to grow old, but I have done so.
On an afternoon like this,
one can age a thousand years
in the moment it takes a dust mote
to swirl through the pooled glow
of a reading lamp at the library,
where the turning pages,
interred in so much stillness,
are leaden with silence.

And in the street outside,
Eternity deepens to teal
as the light, stumbling a little,
marches stridently down to the water.

SO MANY DEATHS

In memoriam.

In those last months Pat's face was already
a funerary mask, stunned synapses flashing
weakly beneath its stillness like lightning
on the edge of a summer storm.
Victor probably never even saw the car
that struck him, killing his Pitbull puppy too.
Sophie's dismembered corpse was found
buried below a hedge in Golden Gate Park.
Jaimes lost ninety pounds in a single week,
reduced to a rasping skeleton the morning
he finally succumbed to Lou Gehrig's disease.
Allison stepped firmly over the international-
orange railing of the bridge, although no one
knows for certain whether she was facing
the skyline as if in some broken farewell
or staring vacantly out to sea. My father's
body, pallid almost to translucence,
slid peacefully into the abyss, his mind
having gone on ahead of him. Mike's cancer
established a foothold in every major organ
before it was detected; in the ambulance
he spewed a fluid as black and heavy as tar.
Cancer took Adrienne as well: Now she lies
under a polished headstone depicting
in intricately carved bas-relief the Bahá'í
temple in Wilmette. Marsha, unlucky in love,
probably hits on angels in the afterlife.
Gentle Carlos Ramirez with his Whitman beard,

who actually wrote his poems on the pliant green
of new leaves, has blown away with the first
brittle bronze of autumn, his words all dust.
So many deaths, my lines can't contain them!
It's cold tonight, although it's early July,
and somewhere out on Nineteenth Avenue
a mournful siren fades as darkness falls.

INDEX OF TITLES

A Brief Geology of Death, 179
A Century Ago, 103
A Faint Combustion in Late Summer Air, 48
A Fragment of the Buddha's Skull, 184
A Ghostly Remnant of a House Now Gone, 127
A Grave I've Never Visited, 77
A Hand-Blown Bottle, 100
A Little Pity Ought To Be Allowed, 52
A Man Selling Whips on Christmas Eve, 200
A Mean, Unpleasant Guy, 37
A Numbness Where My Wedding Ring Once Was, 16
A Parish Church in East Anglia, 35
A Physical Therapist Volunteers in Port-Au-Prince, 55
A Plain Wooden Cross, 116
A Possible Starting Point, 163
A Puzzle Box, 165
A Silence Fills the Craters of the Tongue, 130
A Sort of Mad Salvation, 56
A Winter Sky with Ansel Adams Clouds, 122
After the Flood, 186
Afterimage, 59
Airborne, 185
All Saint's Day, 75
An Old Saw, 178
Answering the Riddle, 146
Apple Trees, 144
April Fish, 79
As If It Mattered Now, 18
At My Father's Deathbed, 20
Audley End, 150

Azure and Indigo, 45
Beulah Rock and the Three-Dollar Turban, 86
Beyond the Veil, 17
Black and White, 63
Bunny Ears, 97
Checking, 167
Cling, If You Must, 170
Closure, 33
Concealed, 191
Concerning Angels, 110
Could He Have Taken Notes, 28
Dad Didn't Waste His Time, 22
Dad Wasn't Much for Protocol, 23
Dance of the Dresses, 158
Dave Van Ronk Was Fond of Tullamore Dew, 121
David Bowie, Natalie Cole, and Igneous Rock, 106
Daybreak in Alabama, 199
Dead Phone Booth, 198
Death Watch, 169
December Overtakes Us, 13
Decoration Day, 166
Dr. Einstein Listens to Barbecue Bob's "Mississippi Heavy Water Blues", 57
Dying Men Prefer Their Privacy, 21
Early November Light, 19
Echoes of Ancient Music, 36
Elijah Rock Contemplates Filling His Father's Footsteps, 98
Empty Stadium at Night, 183
Entering the Tomb, 172
Eternity Deepens to Teal, 201
Every Brown and Withered Winter Lawn, 8
Fickle Weather, 188
Four Clerihews, 192

God Forbid We Disturb the Neighbors, 26
Graffiti, 180
Grandpa's Campaign in Belgium, 42
"He Must Mean His Aunt", 39
Hearses, 151
Henry, Walt, and Bram, 189
Her Happy Lions, Iced in Red, 128
His Last Wishes, 29
Horse Sense, 24
"How about That, Sports Fans?", 25
Kumquat Acquired His Moniker, 96
I Bet You'd Hate This Poem, 51
I Haven't Learned To Love My Solitude, 44
If I Had My Druthers, 159
Igneous Rock among the Lagomorphs, 89
Igneous Rock and Eustace Tubman, 93
Igneous Rock and the Mermaid, 94
Igneous Rock and the Snake Handlers, 101
Igneous Rock As a Pawn of Memory, 117
Igneous Rock Considers Posterity, 102
Igneous Rock in the Wee Small Hours, 105
Igneous Rock Is No Philosopher, 107
Igneous Rock Laments the Last Election, 113
Igneous Rock Peruses the Family Album, 111
Igneous Rock's High School Reunion, 114
Impatiens, 78
In Drenched November, 10
In Less Than Half a Year I Will Be Sixty, 129
Indigenous People's Day, 69
It Will Grow Even Colder Than We Know, 131
Knife Grinder, 154
L. Frank Baum's Final Words, 175
Lazarus Rising, 50

Listening to Dylan on the Muni Metro
a Month after My Father's Death, 12
Lonesome Sentinel, 60
Lullaby and Dirge, 141
Lying in Bed, 196
My Birth-Blind Eyes Invited Nothing In, 64
My Father Lost His Battle with the Lawn, 7
My Father, Near the End, 321
My Father's Ashes, 174
My Shakespeare Student Isn't Showing Up, 46
Myrtle Mae Rock Seldom Thinks of the Lord, 99
New World, 145
No Eulogy Commemorates My Father, 4
No Graves Will Open, 81
No Smoker, 19
Nocturne, 152
Not Getting It, 67
Old Women Wearing Masks, 71
Once the Air Clears, 65
Our Parents May Be Clinically Insane, 53
Palm Sunday, 80
Plague Cemetery, Central London, 62
Primer, 147
Recovering from a Cold, Igneous Rock Unwisely Listens
to Blind Willie Johnson, 104
Renée Lighting a Cigarette, 43
Rising toward Radiance, 171
Scène de Genre, 143
Seventeen Below, 194
Snared, 14
So Many Deaths, 202
Solstice Birthday, 38
Sometimes the Sky Is Pliant, 134

Sturgeon Moon, 3
Such Is Fat(e), 108
Tastes like Chicken, 164
Tear Down the Calendar, 11
That Professor on TV, 95
The Cloaked Eroticism of Rose Windows, 135
The Colossi, 61
The Death of a Beloved Pet, 74
The Denouement, 5
The Dismantled Mansions, 68
The Fallow Heart, 126
The Farthest, 6
The Final Days of These United States, 124
The Flames That Claimed Him, 173
The Flower Burning, 156
The Fool My Father Sometimes Was, 30
The Force Fails To Awaken the Reverend Igneous Rock, 87
The Ground We're Planted In, 47
The Journey to Lubeck, 58
The Last Blacksmith, 181
The Monks of San Durante, 123
The Numb Haul, 9
The Peacemakers, 149
The Poet As Fisherman, 193
The Portrait of Lord Jesus, 109
The Resonance of Anguish, 190
The Return of the Reverend Igneous Rock, 85
The Reverend Igneous Rock Mails His Income Tax, 90
The Reverend Igneous Rock Watches It Rain, 91
The Sculptor's Yard, 132
The Stricken and the Still, 76
The Surrealist in Love, 187
The True Salt of the Earth, 40

The Two Larrys, 41
The Unfinished Throne, 155
The Vacancy He Leaves, 31
The Weather Here Doesn't Count for Much, 176
The Wedding, 139
These Scribbled Lines Are Disinclined To Rage, 49
Through the Window, 177
Time To Think about a Taxi, 70
Trout, 27
True to His Famous Tag Line, 73
Walker, 182
Watching a Blind Man in a Subway Station, 153
Watching the December Rain, 54
We Can't Be Sure, 168
We Cannot Risk Love, 15
Weather Happens in the Present Tense, 72
Wesley Encounters the Pacific Ocean, 66
What I Recall Most Vividly Is Silence, 125
What's Gone Missing, 34
Your Death Still Feels Immediate Today, 133
Your Unfinished Life, 82

ABOUT THE AUTHOR

ROBERT LAVETT SMITH lives in San Francisco. He holds a B.A in French from Oberlin College, where he also studied creative writing with Stuart Friebert and David Young, and an M.A. in English from the University of New Hampshire, studying with Charles Simic and Mekeel McBride. After graduating from UNH, he joined the Master Class at the 92nd Street YMHA in New York City, where he studied with Galway Kinnell. In addition to *Sturgeon Moon*, he has authored four small-press chapbooks and three previous full-length efforts, *Everything Moves With A Disfigured Grace, Smoke In Cold Weather: A Gathering of Sonnets*, and *The Widower Considers Candles.*

A NOTE ON THE FONTS

This book is set in High Tower Text, designed by American type designer Tobias Frere-Jones in 1996 and based on Nicolas Jensen's 1470 Venetian roman. Titles are set in Gotham Black, one of a family of geometric sans-serif digital typefaces modeled on New York City street signs and designed by Frere-Jones in 2000.

www.ingramcontent.com/pod-product-compliance
Lightning Source LLC
LaVergne TN
LVHW091250080426
835510LV00007B/203